MAX LUCADO

LIFE LESSONS *from*

ACTS

Christ's Church in the World

PREPARED BY THE LIVINGSTONE CORPORATION

THOMAS NELSON
Since 1798

Life Lessons from Acts

© 2018 by Max Lucado

Published in Nashville, Tennessee, by Thomas Nelson. Thomas Nelson is a registered trademark of HarperCollins Christian Publishing, Inc.

Produced with the assistance of the Livingstone Corporation (www.livingstonecorp.com). Project staff includes Jake Barton, Joel Bartlett, Andy Culbertson, Mary Horner Collins, and Will Reaves.

Editor: Neil Wilson

Material for the "Inspiration" sections taken from the following books:

Anxious for Nothing. Copyright © 2017 by Max Lucado. Thomas Nelson, a registered trademark of HarperCollins Christian Publishing, Inc., Nashville, Tennessee.

The Applause of Heaven. Copyright © 1990, 1996, 1999 by Max Lucado. Thomas Nelson, a registered trademark of HarperCollins Christian Publishing, Inc., Nashville, Tennessee.

The Great House of God. Copyright © 1997 by Max Lucado. Thomas Nelson, a registered trademark of HarperCollins Christian Publishing, Inc., Nashville, Tennessee.

It's Not About Me. Copyright © 2004 by Max Lucado. Thomas Nelson, a registered trademark of HarperCollins Christian Publishing, Inc., Nashville, Tennessee.

Outlive Your Life. Copyright © 2010 by Max Lucado. Thomas Nelson, a registered trademark of HarperCollins Christian Publishing, Inc., Nashville, Tennessee

Shaped by God (previously published as *On the Anvil*). Copyright © 2001 by Max Lucado. Tyndale House Publishers, Carol Stream, Illinois.

Six Hours One Friday. Copyright © 2004 by Max Lucado. Thomas Nelson, a registered trademark of HarperCollins Christian Publishing, Inc., Nashville, Tennessee.

When God Whispers Your Name. Copyright © 1994, 1999 by Max Lucado. Thomas Nelson, a registered trademark of HarperCollins Christian Publishing, Inc., Nashville, Tennessee.

Thomas Nelson titles may be purchased in bulk for educational, business, fundraising, or sales promotional use. For information, please e-mail SpecialMarkets@ThomasNelson.com.

ISBN 978-0-3100-8638-3

First Printing December 2017 / Printed in the United States of America

CONTENTS

How to Study the Bible   v

Introduction to the Book of Acts   ix

Lesson 1   Jesus Changes Lives *(Acts 2:29–47)*   1

Lesson 2   We Are Witnesses *(Acts 3:1–16)*   11

Lesson 3   Tried and Tested *(Acts 5:17–33)*   19

Lesson 4   Getting Along with Others *(Acts 6:1–15)*   27

Lesson 5   Looking to Jesus *(Acts 7:51–60)*   37

Lesson 6   The Holy Spirit's Leading *(Acts 8:26–40)*   45

Lesson 7   God's Saving Power *(Acts 9:1–20)*   53

Lesson 8   Unity Among Believers *(Acts 10:24–35)*   63

Lesson 9   God's Grace *(Acts 15:1–11)*   71

Lesson 10   Presenting the Gospel *(Acts 17:16–31)*   79

Lesson 11   Facing Problems and Pain *(Acts 20:15–31)*   89

Lesson 12   Living Your Faith *(Acts 27:13–25)*   99

Leader's Guide for Small Groups   107

HOW TO STUDY THE BIBLE

The Bible is a peculiar book. Words crafted in another language. Deeds done in a distant era. Events recorded in a far-off land. Counsel offered to a foreign people. It is a peculiar book.

It's surprising that anyone reads it. It's too old. Some of its writings date back 5,000 years. It's too bizarre. The book speaks of incredible floods, fires, earthquakes, and people with supernatural abilities. It's too radical. The Bible calls for undying devotion to a carpenter who called himself God's Son.

Logic says this book shouldn't survive. Too old, too bizarre, too radical.

The Bible has been banned, burned, scoffed, and ridiculed. Scholars have mocked it as foolish. Kings have branded it as illegal. A thousand times over the grave has been dug and the dirge has begun, but somehow the Bible never stays in the grave. Not only has it survived, but it has also thrived. It is the single most popular book in all of history. It has been the bestselling book in the world for years!

There is no way on earth to explain it. Which perhaps is the only explanation. For the Bible's durability is not found on *earth* but in *heaven*. The millions who have tested its claims and claimed its promises know there is but one answer: the Bible is God's book and God's voice.

As you read it, you would be wise to give some thought to two questions: *What is the purpose of the Bible?* and *How do I study the Bible?* Time spent reflecting on these two issues will greatly enhance your Bible study.

What is the purpose of the Bible?

Let the Bible itself answer that question: "From infancy you have known the Holy Scriptures, which are able to make you wise for salvation through faith in Christ Jesus" (2 Timothy 3:15).

The purpose of the Bible? Salvation. God's highest passion is to get his children home. His book, the Bible, describes his plan of salvation. The purpose of the Bible is to proclaim God's plan and passion to save his children.

This is the reason why this book has endured through the centuries. It dares to tackle the toughest questions about life: *Where do I go after I die? Is there a God? What do I do with my fears?* The Bible is the treasure map that leads to God's highest treasure—eternal life.

But how do you study the Bible? Countless copies of Scripture sit unread on bookshelves and nightstands simply because people don't know how to read it. What can you do to make the Bible real in your life?

The clearest answer is found in the words of Jesus: "Ask and it will be given to you; seek and you will find; knock and the door will be opened to you" (Matthew 7:7).

The first step in understanding the Bible is asking God to help you. Your should read it prayerfully. If anyone understands God's Word, it is because of God and not the reader.

"The Advocate, the Holy Spirit, whom the Father will send in my name, will teach you all things and will remind you of everything I have said to you" (John 14:26).

Before reading the Bible, pray and invite God to speak to you. Don't go to Scripture looking for your idea, but go searching for his.

Not only should you read the Bible prayerfully, but you should also read it carefully. *"Seek and you will find"* is the pledge. The Bible is not a newspaper to be skimmed but rather a mine to be quarried. *"If you look for it as for silver and search for it as for hidden treasure, then you will understand the fear of the LORD and find the knowledge of God"* (Proverbs 2:4–5).

Any worthy find requires effort. The Bible is no exception. To understand the Bible, you don't have to be brilliant, but you must be willing to roll up your sleeves and search.

"Do your best to present yourself to God as one approved, a worker who does not need to be ashamed and who correctly handles the word of truth" (2 Timothy 2:15).

Here's a practical point. Study the Bible a bit at a time. Hunger is not satisfied by eating twenty-one meals in one sitting once a week. The body needs a steady diet to remain strong. So does the soul. When God sent food to his people in the wilderness, he didn't provide loaves already made. Instead, he sent them manna in the shape of *"thin flakes like frost on the ground"* (Exodus 16:14).

God gave manna in limited portions.

God sends spiritual food the same way. He opens the heavens with just enough nutrients for today's hunger. He provides *"a rule for this, a rule for that; a little here, a little there"* (Isaiah 28:10).

Don't be discouraged if your reading reaps a small harvest. Some days a lesser portion is all that is needed. What is important is to search every day for that day's message. A steady diet of God's Word over a lifetime builds a healthy soul and mind.

It's much like the little girl who returned from her first day at school feeling a bit dejected. Her mom asked, "Did you learn anything?"

"Apparently not enough," the girl responded. "I have to go back tomorrow, and the next day, and the next . . . "

Such is the case with learning. And such is the case with Bible study. Understanding comes little by little over a lifetime.

There is a third step in understanding the Bible. After the asking and seeking comes the knocking. After you ask and search, *"knock and the door will be opened to you"* (Matthew 7:7).

To knock is to stand at God's door. To make yourself available. To climb the steps, cross the porch, stand at the doorway, and volunteer.

Knocking goes beyond the realm of thinking and into the realm of acting.

To knock is to ask, *What can I do? How can I obey? Where can I go?*

It's one thing to know what to do. It's another to do it. But for those who do it—those who choose to obey—a special reward awaits them.

"Whoever looks intently into the perfect law that gives freedom, and continues in it—not forgetting what they have heard, but doing it—they will be blessed in what they do" (James 1:25).

What a promise. Blessings come to those who do what they read in God's Word! It's the same with medicine. If you only read the label but ignore the pills, it won't help. It's the same with food. If you only read the recipe but never cook, you won't be fed. And it's the same with the Bible. If you only read the words but never obey, you'll never know the joy God has promised.

Ask. Search. Knock. Simple, isn't it? So why don't you give it a try? If you do, you'll see why the Bible is the most remarkable book in history.

INTRODUCTION TO
The Book of Acts

They aren't the same men.

Oh, I know they look like it. They have the same names. The same faces. The same mannerisms. They look the same. But they aren't. On the surface they appear no different. Peter is still brazen. Nathanael is still reflective. Philip is still calculating.

They look the same. But they aren't. They aren't the same men you read about in the last four books. The fellows you got to know in the Gospels? These are the ones, but they're different.

You'll see it. As you read you'll see it. In their eyes. You hear it in their voices. You feel it in their passion. These men have changed.

As you read you'll wonder—are these the same guys? The ones who doubted in Galilee? The ones who argued in Capernaum? The ones who ran for their lives in Gethsemane? You'll wonder, "Are these the same men?"

The answer is no. They are different. They have stood face-to-face with God. They have sat at the feet of the resurrected King. They are different.

Within them dwells a fire not found on earth. Christ has taught them. The Father has forgiven them. The Spirit indwells them. They are not the same.

And because they are different, so is the world.

Read their adventures and be encouraged. Read their adventures and be listening. What God did for them, he longs to do for you.

AUTHOR AND DATE

Luke, who also wrote the Gospel that bears his name. Luke included few personal details about himself in his writings, but early church historians held that he was a native of Antioch in Syria, and there is evidence that he resided in Troas and was a frequent traveling companion of the apostle Paul (see Acts 16:10–17; 20:5–15; 21:1–18; 27:1–28:16). He is first mentioned in Colossians 4:14, where Paul refers to him as a physician, and he is also mentioned in 2 Timothy 4:11 and Philemon 1:24. It is believed that he wrote his Gospel and the book of Acts c. AD 60.

SITUATION

The book of Acts ends with Paul still in Rome, which has led scholars to conclude that Luke wrote his books from Rome during Paul's imprisonment. In his dedication to "Theophilus" (Acts 1:1), he indicates he composed his former book (his Gospel) to provide a carefully ordered account of the events of Jesus' life and birth of the early church. Luke appears to have written to a primarily non-Jewish audience, for he frequently relates stories of how the disciples and early church leaders came to welcome those from Gentile (non-Jewish) backgrounds.

KEY THEMES

- The foundations of the early church were established in the aftermath of Jesus' resurrection and ascension.
- The Holy Spirit empowered the disciples to spread the gospel into the world as Jesus commanded.

- The first struggle of the gospel was to stand independently of Jewish tradition and faith.
- The sacrifice Jesus made was for all people.

KEY VERSES

"But you will receive power when the Holy Spirit comes on you; and you will be my witnesses in Jerusalem, and in all Judea and Samaria, and to the ends of the earth" (Acts 1:8).

CONTENTS

I. The Gospel in Jerusalem (1:1–7:60)
II. The Gospel in Judea and Samaria (8:1–12:25)
III. The Gospel in the Non-Jewish World (13:1–28:31)

JESUS CHANGES LIVES

When the people heard this, they were cut to the heart and said to Peter and the other apostles, "Brothers, what shall we do?" Peter replied, "Repent and be baptized, every one of you, in the name of Jesus Christ for the forgiveness of your sins."
ACTS 2:37–38

REFLECTION

Community. Unselfish sharing. Unity. These are things we hope to experience in our families, our churches, and our society. Unfortunately, these qualities are often lacking. The book of Acts, titled the "Acts of the Apostles," records the continuation of the story of the disciples after Jesus ascended to heaven. The first followers of Jesus came from different backgrounds yet demonstrated amazing community as the early church was formed. Think about your church. In what ways can you see the transforming power of Jesus' presence?

_____

_____

_____

_____

_____

_____

_____

_____

SITUATION

For almost two months, Jerusalem had been buzzing with plots, a headline crucifixion, rumors of a resurrection, transformed lives, visits from the risen Jesus, and his sudden departure to heaven. After Jesus left his followers gathered to pray in an upper room, and the Holy Spirit showed up! In the early-morning hours of Pentecost, a new sound was heard in the temple courts: Galileans speaking various languages, praising God in tongues other than their own. A crowd gathered. Conclusions were reached. Then one of the disciples stood up and spoke. Peter, the transformed fisherman who had betrayed his Lord, delivered the first sermon, explaining from Scripture who Jesus really was and why he died. The results were remarkable.

OBSERVATION

Read Acts 2:29–47 from the New International
Version or the New King James Version.

NEW INTERNATIONAL VERSION

[29] "Fellow Israelites, I can tell you confidently that the patriarch David died and was buried, and his tomb is here to this day. [30] But he was a prophet and knew that God had promised him on oath that he would place one of his descendants on his throne. [31] Seeing what was to come, he spoke of the resurrection of the Messiah, that he was not abandoned to the realm of the dead, nor did his body see decay. [32] God has raised this Jesus to life, and we are all witnesses of it. [33] Exalted to the right hand of God, he has received from the Father the promised Holy Spirit and has poured out what you now see and hear. [34] For David did not ascend to heaven, and yet he said,

> "'The Lord said to my Lord:
> "Sit at my right hand
> [35] until I make your enemies
> a footstool for your feet."'

[36] "Therefore let all Israel be assured of this: God has made this Jesus, whom you crucified, both Lord and Messiah."

[37] When the people heard this, they were cut to the heart and said to Peter and the other apostles, "Brothers, what shall we do?"

[38] Peter replied, "Repent and be baptized, every one of you, in the name of Jesus Christ for the forgiveness of your sins. And you will receive the gift of the Holy Spirit. [39] The promise is for you and your children and for all who are far off—for all whom the Lord our God will call."

[40] With many other words he warned them; and he pleaded with them, "Save yourselves from this corrupt generation." [41] Those who accepted his message were baptized, and about three thousand were added to their number that day.

⁴² They devoted themselves to the apostles' teaching and to fellowship, to the breaking of bread and to prayer. ⁴³ Everyone was filled with awe at the many wonders and signs performed by the apostles. ⁴⁴ All the believers were together and had everything in common. ⁴⁵ They sold property and possessions to give to anyone who had need. ⁴⁶ Every day they continued to meet together in the temple courts. They broke bread in their homes and ate together with glad and sincere hearts, ⁴⁷ praising God and enjoying the favor of all the people. And the Lord added to their number daily those who were being saved.

New King James Version

²⁹ "Men and brethren, let me speak freely to you of the patriarch David, that he is both dead and buried, and his tomb is with us to this day. ³⁰ Therefore, being a prophet, and knowing that God had sworn with an oath to him that of the fruit of his body, according to the flesh, He would raise up the Christ to sit on his throne, ³¹ he, foreseeing this, spoke concerning the resurrection of the Christ, that His soul was not left in Hades, nor did His flesh see corruption. ³² This Jesus God has raised up, of which we are all witnesses. ³³ Therefore being exalted to the right hand of God, and having received from the Father the promise of the Holy Spirit, He poured out this which you now see and hear.

³⁴ "For David did not ascend into the heavens, but he says himself:

> 'The LORD said to my Lord,
> "Sit at My right hand,
> ³⁵ Till I make Your enemies Your footstool."'

³⁶ "Therefore let all the house of Israel know assuredly that God has made this Jesus, whom you crucified, both Lord and Christ."

³⁷ Now when they heard this, they were cut to the heart, and said to Peter and the rest of the apostles, "Men and brethren, what shall we do?"

³⁸ Then Peter said to them, "Repent, and let every one of you be baptized in the name of Jesus Christ for the remission of sins; and you shall

receive the gift of the Holy Spirit. [39] For the promise is to you and to your children, and to all who are afar off, as many as the Lord our God will call."

[40] And with many other words he testified and exhorted them, saying, "Be saved from this perverse generation." [41] Then those who gladly received his word were baptized; and that day about three thousand souls were added to them. [42] And they continued steadfastly in the apostles' doctrine and fellowship, in the breaking of bread, and in prayers. [43] Then fear came upon every soul, and many wonders and signs were done through the apostles. [44] Now all who believed were together, and had all things in common, [45] and sold their possessions and goods, and divided them among all, as anyone had need.

[46] So continuing daily with one accord in the temple, and breaking bread from house to house, they ate their food with gladness and simplicity of heart, [47] praising God and having favor with all the people. And the Lord added to the church daily those who were being saved.

EXPLORATION

1. What did Peter say about David? How would this have resonated with the crowd?

_____

_____

_____

2. What bold statements did Peter make in his sermon?

_____

_____

3. How did the people react to Peter's declaration?

_____

_____

_____

4. What instructions did Peter give to the people?

5. What did Peter say to the crowds of onlookers about the Holy Spirit?

6. How did the new believers grow in their faith? How did they practice that faith?

INSPIRATION

A transformed group stood beside a transformed Peter as he announced some weeks later: "So, all the people of Israel should know this truly: God has made Jesus—the man you nailed to the cross—both Lord and Christ."

No timidity in his words. No reluctance. About three thousand people believed his message.

The apostles sparked a movement. The people became followers of the death-conqueror. They couldn't hear enough or say enough about him . . . Christ was their model, their message. They preached "Jesus Christ and him crucified," not for the lack of another topic, but because they couldn't exhaust this one.

What unlocked the doors of the apostles' hearts?

Simple. They saw Jesus. They encountered the Christ. Their sins collided with their Savior and their Savior won!

A lot of things would happen to them over the next few decades. Many nights would be spent away from home. Hunger would gnaw at their bellies. Rain would soak their skin. Stones would bruise their bodies. Shipwrecks, lashings, martyrdom. But there was a scene in the repertoire of memories that caused them to never look back: the betrayed coming back to find his betrayers; not to scourge them, but to send them. Not to criticize them for forgetting, but to commission them to remember. *Remember* that he who was dead is alive and they who were guilty have been forgiven. (From *Six Hours One Friday* by Max Lucado.)

REACTION

7. What changes has Jesus made in your life?

8. What circumstances caused you to open your heart to God?

9. Why do you think some people resist the convicting work of the Holy Spirit?

10. The Holy Spirit gave Peter boldness to speak the truth. What ability or gift have you received from God?

11. How have you discovered the spiritual gifts God has given you?

_____

_____

_____

_____

_____

_____

12. How can you use your gifts to help bring others into God's kingdom?

_____

_____

_____

_____

_____

LIFE LESSONS

Authentic followers of Jesus always have company. In fact, if we feel all alone in our faith, one of the explanations may be that we're not following Jesus as closely as we think we are. The first disciples went from feeling all alone to speaking out and discovering more than 3,000 new companions. The practice of faith involves others. So make it a point to pursue healthy relationships with other believers. Ask Jesus to change you into an agent of peace in every situation you find yourself in. Ask him to make you into good company.

DEVOTION

Father, we invite the powerful indwelling of your Spirit, because we know that we do not have the power to change ourselves. May we be open to your convicting work. May we be sincere and willing to grow as you lead us. Father, transform us into your likeness.

JOURNALING

In what area of your life have you resisted the Spirit's work? How can you change that attitude?

FOR FURTHER READING

To complete the book of Acts during this twelve-part study, read Acts 1:1–2:47. For more Bible passages about God's power to change people, read Romans 1:16–17; 8:9–14; 16:17–19; 2 Corinthians 3:18; Galatians 5:22; Ephesians 3:16–20; Colossians 1:10–12; and 2 Peter 1:3.

WE ARE WITNESSES

Then Peter said, "Silver and gold I do not have,
but what I do have I give you: In the name of
Jesus Christ of Nazareth, rise up and walk."
ACTS 3:6 NKJV

REFLECTION

Think back to your life before you knew about Christ. Perhaps you were acutely aware that something was wrong with life. You were missing something. Or maybe you had a vague feeling of unease. Then someone spoke words of truth into your life. Someone witnessed to you about what Jesus meant to him or her. Someone explained who Jesus was. Who helped you understand the truth of the gospel? How did that person accomplish that task?

SITUATION

The days of excitement and new faith in the early church made the apostles' lives hectic and full. They had to stay focused. There were great spiritual and physical needs everywhere. One day, Peter and John had an eye-opening encounter with a crippled man. He was merely hoping for some financial help, but the apostles gave him something far better.

OBSERVATION

Read Acts 3:1–16 from the New International Version or the New King James Version.

NEW INTERNATIONAL VERSION
¹ One day Peter and John were going up to the temple at the time of prayer—at three in the afternoon. ² Now a man who was lame from birth was being carried to the temple gate called Beautiful, where he was put every day to beg from those going into the temple courts. ³ When he saw

Peter and John about to enter, he asked them for money. [4] Peter looked straight at him, as did John. Then Peter said, "Look at us!" [5] So the man gave them his attention, expecting to get something from them.

[6] Then Peter said, "Silver or gold I do not have, but what I do have I give you. In the name of Jesus Christ of Nazareth, walk." [7] Taking him by the right hand, he helped him up, and instantly the man's feet and ankles became strong. [8] He jumped to his feet and began to walk. Then he went with them into the temple courts, walking and jumping, and praising God. [9] When all the people saw him walking and praising God, [10] they recognized him as the same man who used to sit begging at the temple gate called Beautiful, and they were filled with wonder and amazement at what had happened to him.

[11] While the man held on to Peter and John, all the people were astonished and came running to them in the place called Solomon's Colonnade. [12] When Peter saw this, he said to them: "Fellow Israelites, why does this surprise you? Why do you stare at us as if by our own power or godliness we had made this man walk? [13] The God of Abraham, Isaac and Jacob, the God of our fathers, has glorified his servant Jesus. You handed him over to be killed, and you disowned him before Pilate, though he had decided to let him go. [14] You disowned the Holy and Righteous One and asked that a murderer be released to you. [15] You killed the author of life, but God raised him from the dead. We are witnesses of this. [16] By faith in the name of Jesus, this man whom you see and know was made strong. It is Jesus' name and the faith that comes through him that has completely healed him, as you can all see.

New King James Version

[1] Now Peter and John went up together to the temple at the hour of prayer, the ninth hour. [2] And a certain man lame from his mother's womb was carried, whom they laid daily at the gate of the temple which is called Beautiful, to ask alms from those who entered the temple; [3] who, seeing Peter and John about to go into the temple, asked for alms. [4] And fixing his eyes on him, with John, Peter said, "Look at us." [5] So he gave them his attention, expecting to receive something from them. [6] Then Peter said, "Silver and gold I do not have, but what I do have I give you: In the name

of Jesus Christ of Nazareth, rise up and walk." ⁷ And he took him by the right hand and lifted him up, and immediately his feet and ankle bones received strength. ⁸ So he, leaping up, stood and walked and entered the temple with them—walking, leaping, and praising God. ⁹ And all the people saw him walking and praising God. ¹⁰ Then they knew that it was he who sat begging alms at the Beautiful Gate of the temple; and they were filled with wonder and amazement at what had happened to him.

¹¹ Now as the lame man who was healed held on to Peter and John, all the people ran together to them in the porch which is called Solomon's, greatly amazed. ¹² So when Peter saw it, he responded to the people: "Men of Israel, why do you marvel at this? Or why look so intently at us, as though by our own power or godliness we had made this man walk? ¹³ The God of Abraham, Isaac, and Jacob, the God of our fathers, glorified His Servant Jesus, whom you delivered up and denied in the presence of Pilate, when he was determined to let Him go. ¹⁴ But you denied the Holy One and the Just, and asked for a murderer to be granted to you, ¹⁵ and killed the Prince of life, whom God raised from the dead, of which we are witnesses. ¹⁶ And His name, through faith in His name, has made this man strong, whom you see and know. Yes, the faith which comes through Him has given him this perfect soundness in the presence of you all.

EXPLORATION

1. What was the crippled man's life like before he met Peter and John?

---

2. What were Peter and John unable to give the crippled man? What did they give instead?

---

3. How did the crippled man react to the miracle?

_____

_____

_____

4. How did the people at the temple respond to Peter and John after they heard about the miracle?

_____

_____

_____

5. What opportunity did this miracle provide for Peter?

_____

_____

_____

6. How did Peter explain the healing of the crippled man?

_____

_____

_____

INSPIRATION

This word *compassion* is one of the oddest in Scripture. The New Testament Greek lexicon says this word means "to be moved as to one's bowels . . . (for the bowels were thought to be the seat of love and pity)." It shares a root system with *splanchnology*, the study of the visceral parts. Compassion, then, is a movement deep within—a kick in the gut.

Perhaps that is why we often turn away. Who can bear such an emotion? Especially when we can do nothing about it. Why look suffering in the face if we can't make a difference? Yet what if we could? What if our attention could reduce someone's pain? This is the promise of the encounter.

"Then Peter said, 'Silver or gold I do not have, but what I do have I give you. In the name of Jesus Christ of Nazareth, walk.' Taking him by the right hand, he helped him up, and instantly the man's feet and ankles became strong" (Acts 3:6–7). What if Peter had said, "Since I don't have any silver or gold, I'll keep my mouth shut"? But he didn't. He placed his mustard-seed sized deed (a look and a touch) in the soil of God's love. And look what happened.

The thick, meaty hand of the fisherman reached for the frail, thin one of the beggar. Think Sistine Chapel and the high hand of God. One from above, the other from below. A holy helping hand. Peter lifted the man toward himself. The cripple swayed like a newborn calf finding its balance. It appeared as if the man would fall, but he didn't. He stood. And as he stood, he began to shout, and passersby began to stop. They stopped and watched. . . .

An honest look led to a helping hand that led to a conversation about eternity. Works done in God's name long outlive our earthly lives.

Let's be the people who stop at the gate. Let's look at the hurting until we hurt with them. No hurrying past, turning away, or shifting of eyes. No pretending or glossing over. Let's look at the face until we see the person. (From *Outlive Your Life* by Max Lucado.)

REACTION

7. What can you learn from Peter's example about spreading the gospel?

---

8. Why is it important for believers to encourage others to follow Jesus?

---

9. What does it mean to be *bold* witnesses for Christ?

10. What excuses do Christians often use to keep quiet about their faith?

11. What steps can you take to prepare yourself to explain the gospel to others?

12. Think of one person in your life who does not know Christ. When can you share the gospel with that person?

LIFE LESSONS

Witnessing is simply sharing what you have seen. Start each day with a heartfelt request: "Lord, send someone my way today whose need is so obvious that even I can't miss it! Remind me that what I have in you is the very best gift I could give that person, no matter what he or she has asked of me. And when I meet that person, help me resist the temptation to come up with something witty to say, but to instead simply depend on you for what to say."

DEVOTION

Father, you give us many opportunities to proclaim your salvation message, yet we often shirk back from those opportunities in fearful silence. Forgive us, Father. Fill us with courage to boldly speak the truth in love. Teach us what it means to be your witnesses.

JOURNALING

How have you used the opportunities God has given you to share the gospel?

_____

_____

_____

_____

_____

_____

_____

_____

_____

_____

_____

_____

FOR FURTHER READING

To complete the book of Acts during this twelve-part study, read Acts 3:1–4:37. For more Bible passages about witnessing, read Mark 5:19; 16:15; Acts 1:8; 2 Corinthians 4:13–14; Colossians 4:5–6; 2 Timothy 4:2; and 1 Peter 3:15–16.

TRIED AND TESTED

Peter and the other apostles replied: "We must obey God rather than human beings! The God of our ancestors raised Jesus from the dead—whom you killed by hanging him on a cross."

ACTS 5:29–30

REFLECTION

Jesus said that his followers would experience tough times. "If they hated me, they'll hate you too," he said. Being bold and "out there" about your faith is not easy—and it wasn't easy for the early Christians either. Their boldness landed them in some pretty hot water. Think of someone you know who has suffered hardship, opposition, or worse because of his or her faith. What do you admire about that person?

SITUATION

In the aftermath of Jesus' resurrection, the message about forgiveness and new life seemed unstoppable. Boldness bred popularity. But it also provoked a jealous backlash. The religious establishment in Jerusalem felt threatened by these brash Jesus-followers. So they decided to try intimidation as a tactic to silence those most prominent in spreading the news about Jesus.

OBSERVATION

Read Acts 5:17–33 from the New International Version or the New King James Version.

NEW INTERNATIONAL VERSION

[17] Then the high priest and all his associates, who were members of the party of the Sadducees, were filled with jealousy. [18] They arrested the apostles and put them in the public jail. [19] But during the night an angel of

the Lord opened the doors of the jail and brought them out. [20] "Go, stand in the temple courts," he said, "and tell the people all about this new life."

[21] At daybreak they entered the temple courts, as they had been told, and began to teach the people.

When the high priest and his associates arrived, they called together the Sanhedrin—the full assembly of the elders of Israel—and sent to the jail for the apostles. [22] But on arriving at the jail, the officers did not find them there. So they went back and reported, [23] "We found the jail securely locked, with the guards standing at the doors; but when we opened them, we found no one inside." [24] On hearing this report, the captain of the temple guard and the chief priests were at a loss, wondering what this might lead to.

[25] Then someone came and said, "Look! The men you put in jail are standing in the temple courts teaching the people." [26] At that, the captain went with his officers and brought the apostles. They did not use force, because they feared that the people would stone them.

[27] The apostles were brought in and made to appear before the Sanhedrin to be questioned by the high priest. [28] "We gave you strict orders not to teach in this name," he said. "Yet you have filled Jerusalem with your teaching and are determined to make us guilty of this man's blood."

[29] Peter and the other apostles replied: "We must obey God rather than human beings! [30] The God of our ancestors raised Jesus from the dead—whom you killed by hanging him on a cross. [31] God exalted him to his own right hand as Prince and Savior that he might bring Israel to repentance and forgive their sins. [32] We are witnesses of these things, and so is the Holy Spirit, whom God has given to those who obey him."

[33] When they heard this, they were furious and wanted to put them to death.

New King James Version

[17] Then the high priest rose up, and all those who were with him (which is the sect of the Sadducees), and they were filled with indignation, [18] and laid their hands on the apostles and put them in the common prison. [19] But at night an angel of the Lord opened the prison doors and brought

them out, and said, ²⁰ "Go, stand in the temple and speak to the people all the words of this life."

²¹ And when they heard that, they entered the temple early in the morning and taught. But the high priest and those with him came and called the council together, with all the elders of the children of Israel, and sent to the prison to have them brought.

²² But when the officers came and did not find them in the prison, they returned and reported, ²³ saying, "Indeed we found the prison shut securely, and the guards standing outside before the doors; but when we opened them, we found no one inside!" ²⁴ Now when the high priest, the captain of the temple, and the chief priests heard these things, they wondered what the outcome would be. ²⁵ So one came and told them, saying, "Look, the men whom you put in prison are standing in the temple and teaching the people!"

²⁶ Then the captain went with the officers and brought them without violence, for they feared the people, lest they should be stoned. ²⁷ And when they had brought them, they set them before the council. And the high priest asked them, ²⁸ saying, "Did we not strictly command you not to teach in this name? And look, you have filled Jerusalem with your doctrine, and intend to bring this Man's blood on us!"

²⁹ But Peter and the other apostles answered and said: "We ought to obey God rather than men. ³⁰ The God of our fathers raised up Jesus whom you murdered by hanging on a tree. ³¹ Him God has exalted to His right hand to be Prince and Savior, to give repentance to Israel and forgiveness of sins. ³² And we are His witnesses to these things, and so also is the Holy Spirit whom God has given to those who obey Him."

³³ When they heard this, they were furious and plotted to kill them.

EXPLORATION

1. What was the problem between the apostles and the religious leaders?

---

2. How did the high priest try to stop the disciples from preaching?

3. How were the disciples able to continue their ministry?

4. What accusations did the high priest make against Peter and the other apostles when they were found preaching about Jesus a second time?

5. How did the apostles deal with this opposition from the religious leaders?

6. What claims did Peter and the apostles make that so infuriated the Jewish leaders?

INSPIRATION

On God's anvil. Perhaps you've been there. Melted down. Formless. Undone.

I know. I've been on it. It's rough. It's a spiritual slump, a famine. The fire goes out. Although the fire may flame for a moment, it soon disappears. We drift downward. Downward into the foggy valley of question, the misty lowland of discouragement. Motivation wanes. Desire is distant. Responsibilities are depressing.

Passion? It slips out the door. Enthusiasm? Are you kidding? Anvil time.

It can be caused by a death, a breakup, going broke, going prayerless. The light switch is flipped off and the room darkens . . .

On the anvil.

Brought face to face with God out of the utter realization that we have nowhere else to go. Jesus, in the Garden. Peter, with a tear-streamed face. David, after Bathsheba. Elijah and the "still, small voice." Paul, blind in Damascus.

Pound, pound, pound.

I hope you're not on the anvil. (Unless you need to be and, if so, I hope you are.) Anvil time is not to be avoided; it's to be experienced. Although the tunnel is dark, it does go through the mountain. Anvil time reminds us of who we are and who God is. We shouldn't try to escape it. To escape it could be to escape God.

God sees our life from beginning to end. He may lead us through a storm at age thirty so we can endure a hurricane at age sixty. An instrument is useful only if it's in the right shape. A dull ax or a bent screwdriver needs attention, and so do we. A good blacksmith keeps his tools in shape. So does God.

Should God place you on his anvil, be thankful. It means he thinks you're still worth reshaping. (From *Shaped by God* by Max Lucado.)

REACTION

7. What do people usually do when life gets difficult?

---

8. What lessons can be learned from experiencing pain?

---

9. What good has come from a difficult experience in your life?

_____

_____

_____

10. What opposition do believers face today?

_____

_____

_____

11. What can you learn from the apostles' example about coping with criticism and unfair treatment?

_____

_____

_____

_____

12. How can you develop a joyful spirit in the midst of trials?

_____

_____

_____

_____

LIFE LESSONS

We like the idea of being used by God, but often dislike the measures God takes to prepare us for service. We like the idea of doing God's work, but dislike the reality of how much God's work will cost us. Jesus told us to count the cost (see Luke 14:25–33). We like the pleasure of knowing God, but dislike the pressure that comes from knowing God. Jesus compared the experience of following him to the task of carrying a cross. Gotten many slivers lately? If so, don't lose hope. Nothing is ever wasted, and God will never leave you.

DEVOTION

Father, we believe that when we meet you face-to-face, any trials that we endured on this earth will seem small. Help us to focus on matters of eternity and be bold in sharing the message of Christ. And please help us to remember that any earthly struggle is small in comparison to the great God we serve.

JOURNALING

How do you need to change your attitude toward problems and difficulties in your life?

FOR FURTHER READING

To complete the book of Acts during this twelve-part study, read Acts 5:1–42. For more Bible passages about trials and testing, read Job 23:10; Psalm 66:10; Isaiah 48:10; 2 Corinthians 4:16–18; Hebrews 10:32–34; James 1:2–4; 5:10–11; and 1 Peter 2:20–21; 4:12–19; 5:10.

GETTING ALONG WITH OTHERS

The twelve summoned the multitude of the disciples and said, "It is not desirable that we should leave the word of God and serve tables. Therefore, brethren, seek out from among you seven men of good reputation, full of the Holy Spirit and wisdom, whom we may appoint over this business."
ACTS 6:2–3 NKJV

REFLECTION

From an early age, most of us were taught about how to get along with others. If we were blessed with siblings, one of the first words we learned to say was "mine," and one of the first things our parents tried to teach us was "share." But sharing and serving don't come naturally, for most of us are pretty self-centered. What is the best advice you've heard about getting along with people? How have you put it into practice?

SITUATION

Even the best plan has flaws. Human responses, even the best intentioned, can still leave some needs unmet. As the community of followers of Jesus expanded, certain challenges naturally developed. These challenges may have revealed deeper racial and social issues in the community, but the presenting problem had to do with one group's basic needs and someone being willing to serve. The apostles were asked to solve this practical problem. Note how they gave the responsibility back to the people.

OBSERVATION

*Read Acts 6:1–15 from the New International
Version or the New King James Version.*

New International Version

[1] In those days when the number of disciples was increasing, the Hellenistic Jews among them complained against the Hebraic Jews because their widows were being overlooked in the daily distribution of food. [2] So the

Twelve gathered all the disciples together and said, "It would not be right for us to neglect the ministry of the word of God in order to wait on tables. ³ Brothers and sisters, choose seven men from among you who are known to be full of the Spirit and wisdom. We will turn this responsibility over to them ⁴ and will give our attention to prayer and the ministry of the word."

⁵ This proposal pleased the whole group. They chose Stephen, a man full of faith and of the Holy Spirit; also Philip, Procorus, Nicanor, Timon, Parmenas, and Nicolas from Antioch, a convert to Judaism. ⁶ They presented these men to the apostles, who prayed and laid their hands on them.

⁷ So the word of God spread. The number of disciples in Jerusalem increased rapidly, and a large number of priests became obedient to the faith.

⁸ Now Stephen, a man full of God's grace and power, performed great wonders and signs among the people. ⁹ Opposition arose, however, from members of the Synagogue of the Freedmen (as it was called)—Jews of Cyrene and Alexandria as well as the provinces of Cilicia and Asia—who began to argue with Stephen. ¹⁰ But they could not stand up against the wisdom the Spirit gave him as he spoke.

¹¹ Then they secretly persuaded some men to say, "We have heard Stephen speak blasphemous words against Moses and against God."

¹² So they stirred up the people and the elders and the teachers of the law. They seized Stephen and brought him before the Sanhedrin. ¹³ They produced false witnesses, who testified, "This fellow never stops speaking against this holy place and against the law. ¹⁴ For we have heard him say that this Jesus of Nazareth will destroy this place and change the customs Moses handed down to us."

¹⁵ All who were sitting in the Sanhedrin looked intently at Stephen, and they saw that his face was like the face of an angel.

NEW KING JAMES VERSION

¹ Now in those days, when the number of the disciples was multiplying, there arose a complaint against the Hebrews by the Hellenists, because their widows were neglected in the daily distribution. ² Then the twelve

summoned the multitude of the disciples and said, "It is not desirable that we should leave the word of God and serve tables. ³ Therefore, brethren, seek out from among you seven men of good reputation, full of the Holy Spirit and wisdom, whom we may appoint over this business; ⁴ but we will give ourselves continually to prayer and to the ministry of the word."

⁵ And the saying pleased the whole multitude. And they chose Stephen, a man full of faith and the Holy Spirit, and Philip, Prochorus, Nicanor, Timon, Parmenas, and Nicolas, a proselyte from Antioch, ⁶ whom they set before the apostles; and when they had prayed, they laid hands on them.

⁷ Then the word of God spread, and the number of the disciples multiplied greatly in Jerusalem, and a great many of the priests were obedient to the faith.

⁸ And Stephen, full of faith and power, did great wonders and signs among the people. ⁹ Then there arose some from what is called the Synagogue of the Freedmen (Cyrenians, Alexandrians, and those from Cilicia and Asia), disputing with Stephen. ¹⁰ And they were not able to resist the wisdom and the Spirit by which he spoke. ¹¹ Then they secretly induced men to say, "We have heard him speak blasphemous words against Moses and God." ¹² And they stirred up the people, the elders, and the scribes; and they came upon him, seized him, and brought him to the council. ¹³ They also set up false witnesses who said, "This man does not cease to speak blasphemous words against this holy place and the law; ¹⁴ for we have heard him say that this Jesus of Nazareth will destroy this place and change the customs which Moses delivered to us." ¹⁵ And all who sat in the council, looking steadfastly at him, saw his face as the face of an angel.

EXPLORATION

1. What problem arose in the early church regarding people's needs?

_____

_____

_____

_____

2. What solution did the apostles offer? Why didn't they volunteer to *be* the solution?

_____

_____

_____

_____

3. How did the group respond to the apostles' idea?

_____

_____

_____

_____

4. What does this passage reveal about Stephen's character and relationship with God?

_____

_____

_____

_____

5. How did God use Stephen to help the early church?

_____

_____

_____

_____

6. How did the Jews from the "Synagogue of the Freedmen" try to stop Stephen's work?

_____

_____

_____

_____

INSPIRATION

Rapid church growth brought needy people, and among the needy people were widows. They had no source of income. When they buried their husbands, they buried their financial security. Government support? Company pension? The Widows Job Corp? Didn't exist. According to the culture of their day, the extended family provided support. But extended families disowned Christian relatives, leaving the widows of the church with only one place to turn: the church. The congregation responded with a daily distribution of food, clothing, and money.

That's when the trouble began. The Greek-speaking widows were overlooked. Why? They were outsiders. Immigrants. These women didn't grow up in Judea or Galilee. They hailed from the distant lands of Greece, Rome, and Syria. If they spoke Aramaic at all, they did so with an accent.

Consequently, they were "neglected in the daily distribution" (Acts 6:1 NKJV). The driver of the Meals on Wheels truck skipped their houses. The manager of the food pantry permitted Hebrew women the first pick. The food bank director separated requests into two stacks: locals and immigrants.

How did the church respond? I'm picturing a called meeting of the apostles, a circle of bearded faces: Andrew, John, Peter, Thomas, and the others. They heard the concerns of the women and pondered their options. They could dismiss them entirely. They could ignore the needy, neglect the neglected. After all, the apostles were spiritual leaders. They fed souls, not stomachs. They dealt in matters of sin and salvation, not sandals and soup. Couldn't they dismiss the disparity as an unnecessary concern? They could, except for one problem. Their Master didn't. . . .

The first church meeting led to the first task force. The apostles unleashed their best people on their biggest problem. The challenge demands this. "Poverty," as Rich Stearns, president of World Vision in the United States, told me, "is rocket science." Simple solutions simply don't exist. Most of us don't know what to do about the avalanche of national debt, the withholding of lifesaving medicines, the corruption at the seaports, and the abduction of children. Most of us don't know what to do, but someone does!

Some people are pouring every ounce of God-given wisdom into the resolution of these problems. We need specialist organizations, such as World Vision, Compassion International, Living Water, and International Justice Mission. We need our brightest and best to continue the legacy of the Jerusalem task force of Acts 6. (From *Outlive Your Life* by Max Lucado.)

REACTION

7. What are some things that cause tension and disagreements in the church today?

_____

_____

_____

8. Why is it important for Christians to get along with one another?

_____

_____

_____

9. What can you learn from the early church leaders about resolving differences?

_____

_____

_____

10. What happens when believers criticize and argue with one another?

_____

_____

_____

11. What character traits do believers need to possess to get along with one another?

_____

_____

_____

_____

_____

12. How can you and your church better cultivate these qualities?

_____

_____

_____

_____

LIFE LESSONS

Life isn't measured by how many problems we have but by how we respond to them. That's what we can learn from the apostles as they formed the first church. They were starting a brand new thing, and there was no model for them to follow. Challenges and disagreements were bound to happen. They chose to work together to overcome the problems. We can too. When Jesus informed us that we would have trouble (see John 16:33), he did not give us permission to be overcome by trouble, but to accept his help to overcome it!

DEVOTION

Father, we pray that your church would be unified in love and purpose. Teach us how to sow seeds of peace and harmony. Help us to overcome trouble not by blaming others but by counting on you! Help us to resolve our differences lovingly, so that unbelievers are drawn into your family because of the love we share. Teach us to think more in terms of "it's not about me."

JOURNALING

What do you usually do when you feel tension in a relationship? How can you improve the way you resolve conflicts with others?

FOR FURTHER READING

To complete the book of Acts during this twelve-part study, read Acts 6:1–15. For more Bible passages about getting along with people, read Proverbs 17:14; Romans 12:16; 1 Corinthians 1:10; 6:1–7; Ephesians 4:2–4; Philippians 2:3–4; 1 Thessalonians 5:12–15; and 1 Peter 3:8–9.

LOOKING TO JESUS

*Stephen, full of the Holy Spirit, looked up to heaven and
saw the glory of God, and Jesus standing at the right
hand of God. "Look," he said, "I see heaven open and
the Son of Man standing at the right hand of God."*

ACTS 7:55–56

REFLECTION

As Christians, our aim is to live and die for God's glory. By looking to Jesus for grace and mercy, we can face the tough times of life. Think about someone that you know who has faced a life-threatening situation with faith and courage. What do you learn from this person?

_____

_____

_____

_____

SITUATION

Stephen didn't have the reputation that surrounded the original disciples. The religious establishment feared the popularity of the apostles, but they decided Stephen was expendable. So when he began to teach, they put him on trial. False witnesses were hired to create a case. Stephen made an impassioned statement, not so much in his own defense but to urge his opponents to give Jesus serious consideration. As he neared the end of his remarks—and his life—Stephen made some lasting statements that are worth pondering.

OBSERVATION

*Read Acts 7:51–60 from the New International
Version or the New King James Version.*

NEW INTERNATIONAL VERSION
⁵¹ "You stiff-necked people! Your hearts and ears are still uncircumcised. You are just like your ancestors: You always resist the Holy Spirit! ⁵² Was there ever a prophet your ancestors did not persecute? They even killed those who predicted the coming of the Righteous One. And now you

have betrayed and murdered him— [53] you who have received the law that was given through angels but have not obeyed it."

[54] When the members of the Sanhedrin heard this, they were furious and gnashed their teeth at him. [55] But Stephen, full of the Holy Spirit, looked up to heaven and saw the glory of God, and Jesus standing at the right hand of God. [56] "Look," he said, "I see heaven open and the Son of Man standing at the right hand of God."

[57] At this they covered their ears and, yelling at the top of their voices, they all rushed at him, [58] dragged him out of the city and began to stone him. Meanwhile, the witnesses laid their coats at the feet of a young man named Saul.

[59] While they were stoning him, Stephen prayed, "Lord Jesus, receive my spirit." [60] Then he fell on his knees and cried out, "Lord, do not hold this sin against them." When he had said this, he fell asleep.

NEW KING JAMES VERSION

[51] "You stiff-necked and uncircumcised in heart and ears! You always resist the Holy Spirit; as your fathers did, so do you. [52] Which of the prophets did your fathers not persecute? And they killed those who foretold the coming of the Just One, of whom you now have become the betrayers and murderers, [53] who have received the law by the direction of angels and have not kept it."

[54] When they heard these things they were cut to the heart, and they gnashed at him with their teeth. [55] But he, being full of the Holy Spirit, gazed into heaven and saw the glory of God, and Jesus standing at the right hand of God, [56] and said, "Look! I see the heavens opened and the Son of Man standing at the right hand of God!"

[57] Then they cried out with a loud voice, stopped their ears, and ran at him with one accord; [58] and they cast him out of the city and stoned him. And the witnesses laid down their clothes at the feet of a young man named Saul. [59] And they stoned Stephen as he was calling on God and saying, "Lord Jesus, receive my spirit." [60] Then he knelt down and cried out with a loud voice, "Lord, do not charge them with this sin." And when he had said this, he fell asleep.

EXPLORATION

1. What accusations did Stephen make against the members of the ruling council?

_____

_____

_____

2. What comparisons did Stephen make about the religious leaders and their ancestors?

_____

_____

_____

3. What did Stephen mean when he asked, "Was there ever a prophet your ancestors did not persecute" (verse 52)?

_____

_____

_____

_____

4. Why did Stephen's speech infuriate his adversaries?

_____

_____

_____

5. How did Stephen face his impending death? To whom did he look?

_____

_____

_____

6. What do Stephen's last words reveal about his character?

INSPIRATION

Stephen caused a stir before he even opened his mouth. "All who were sitting in the Sanhedrin looked intently at Stephen, and they saw that his face was like the face of an angel" (Acts 6:15). Glowing cheeks. Light pouring through the pores of his face. Did his beard shimmer? Did heaven bathe him in a tunnel of brightness? I don't know how to imagine the scene. But I know how to interpret it. This was God speaking. The sermon emerges, not from Stephen's mind, but from God's heart. Every vowel, consonant, and clearing of the throat was his. This was no casual message.

Nor was it a lightweight message. Fifty-two verses that led the listeners from Abraham to Jesus. Two thousand years of Hebrew history resulted in one indictment: "You're forgetting who holds you." . . . Stephen challenged their big heads with a huge point: *You've forgotten how big God is.* . . .

The council stood in anger. They "gnashed their teeth at him" (Acts 7:54). They bared their fangs like angry jackals pouncing on fresh meat. "They covered their ears and, yelling at the top of their voices, they all rushed at him, dragged him out of the city and began to stone him" (verses 57–58).

Frightening thing, this pride. It would rather kill the truth than consider it. Doesn't it sneak up on us? We begin spiritual journeys as small people. The act of conversion is a humbling one. We confess sins, beg for mercy, bend our knees. We let someone lower us into the waters of baptism. We begin as self-effacing souls. . . .

Gradually our big God changes us. And, gratefully, we lust less, love more, lash out less, look heavenward more. We pay bills, pay attention to spouses, pay respect to parents. People notice the difference. They applaud us. Promote us. Admire us. Appoint us. We dare to outlive our lives. We—who came to Christ as sinful, soiled, and small—accomplish things. We build orphanages, lead companies, deliver the confused out of depression and the sick out of disease. Why, we even write books. We don't feel so small anymore. People talk to us as if we are something special.

"You have great influence."

"What strong faith you have."

"We need mighty saints like you."

Feels nice. Kudos become ladder rungs, and we begin to elevate ourselves. We shed our smallness, discard the Clark Kent glasses, and don a Superman swagger. We forget. We forget who brought us here. . . . Take time to remember. "Look at what you were when God called you" (1 Corinthians 1:26 NCV). Remember who held you in the beginning. Remember who holds you today. (From *Outlive Your Life* by Max Lucado.)

REACTION

7. Why do you think Stephen was able to face death courageously?

---

8. How does Stephen's example encourage you?

---

9. Why do people tend to look to themselves for strength rather than depending on God?

---

10. Where do you usually turn for help when you are in trouble?

_____

_____

_____

11. What happens when you depend on yourself or others to carry you through painful times?

_____

_____

_____

_____

12. What was one specific instance when you received God's help during a difficult time?

_____

_____

_____

_____

LIFE LESSONS

When the crisis moments come . . . when death looms . . . when dreams and plans suddenly disappear—to whom do we turn? Almost every day provides us with small and large opportunities to trust and reach for Jesus' hand. We are most likely to reach for him in our final moments before death if we've been in the habit of doing that all our lives.

DEVOTION

Father, put your hands and your arms around us and embrace us. Carry us through the valleys and give us strength for today and courage for tomorrow. Help us to keep our eyes on you, put aside our pride, and operate in your will. Teach us to reach out and seek you in all things.

JOURNALING

In what area of your life do you need Jesus' help? How can you show your dependence on him?

_____

_____

_____

_____

_____

_____

_____

_____

_____

_____

_____

_____

_____

_____

_____

_____

_____

_____

_____

FOR FURTHER READING

To complete the book of Acts during this twelve-part study, read Acts 7:1–60. For more Bible passages about turning to God, read Psalms 34:5; 105:4; 142:5–6; Acts 3:19; Hebrews 3:1; 12:2; and 1 Peter 5:9.

THE HOLY SPIRIT'S LEADING

Now an angel of the Lord spoke to Philip, saying, "Arise and go toward the south along the road which goes down from Jerusalem to Gaza." This is desert. So he arose and went.

ACTS 8:26–27 NKJV

REFLECTION

Some of life's best experiences begin unexpectedly. Great opportunities to help someone or work together on a project might be waiting just around the bend. It's possible these moments might happen more often if we listened carefully to how God is leading us. Think of a time in your own life when you felt compelled to help someone. What did you do to help that person? How would you describe that moment as a divine encounter that God arranged?

SITUATION

Two men named Philip appear in the accounts of the early church. One was a disciple of Christ, and the other was a man chosen along with Stephen to serve as one of the deacons. Like Stephen, Philip had a way with people. He was also sensitive to God's leading. So it was that he found himself walking along a major road leading south from Jerusalem, through Gaza, toward Egypt and Ethiopia. When he heard the sounds of a traveling caravan behind him, he quickly discovered that God had arranged a special appointment for him.

OBSERVATION

Read Acts 8:26–40 from the New International Version or the New King James Version.

NEW INTERNATIONAL VERSION

26 Now an angel of the Lord said to Philip, "Go south to the road—the desert road—that goes down from Jerusalem to Gaza." 27 So he started

out, and on his way he met an Ethiopian eunuch, an important official in charge of all the treasury of the Kandake (which means "queen of the Ethiopians"). This man had gone to Jerusalem to worship, 28 and on his way home was sitting in his chariot reading the Book of Isaiah the prophet. 29 The Spirit told Philip, "Go to that chariot and stay near it."

30 Then Philip ran up to the chariot and heard the man reading Isaiah the prophet. "Do you understand what you are reading?" Philip asked.

31 "How can I," he said, "unless someone explains it to me?" So he invited Philip to come up and sit with him.

32 This is the passage of Scripture the eunuch was reading:

> "He was led like a sheep to the slaughter,
>   and as a lamb before its shearer is silent,
>   so he did not open his mouth.
> 33 In his humiliation he was deprived of justice.
>   Who can speak of his descendants?
>   For his life was taken from the earth."

34 The eunuch asked Philip, "Tell me, please, who is the prophet talking about, himself or someone else?" 35 Then Philip began with that very passage of Scripture and told him the good news about Jesus.

36 As they traveled along the road, they came to some water and the eunuch said, "Look, here is water. What can stand in the way of my being baptized?"[37] 38 And he gave orders to stop the chariot. Then both Philip and the eunuch went down into the water and Philip baptized him. 39 When they came up out of the water, the Spirit of the Lord suddenly took Philip away, and the eunuch did not see him again, but went on his way rejoicing. 40 Philip, however, appeared at Azotus and traveled about, preaching the gospel in all the towns until he reached Caesarea.

New King James Version

26 Now an angel of the Lord spoke to Philip, saying, "Arise and go toward the south along the road which goes down from Jerusalem to Gaza." This

is desert. ²⁷ So he arose and went. And behold, a man of Ethiopia, a eunuch of great authority under Candace the queen of the Ethiopians, who had charge of all her treasury, and had come to Jerusalem to worship, ²⁸ was returning. And sitting in his chariot, he was reading Isaiah the prophet. ²⁹ Then the Spirit said to Philip, "Go near and overtake this chariot."

³⁰ So Philip ran to him, and heard him reading the prophet Isaiah, and said, "Do you understand what you are reading?"

³¹ And he said, "How can I, unless someone guides me?" And he asked Philip to come up and sit with him. ³² The place in the Scripture which he read was this:

> "He was led as a sheep to the slaughter;
> And as a lamb before its shearer is silent,
> So He opened not His mouth.
> ³³ In His humiliation His justice was taken away,
> And who will declare His generation?
> For His life is taken from the earth."

³⁴ So the eunuch answered Philip and said, "I ask you, of whom does the prophet say this, of himself or of some other man?" ³⁵ Then Philip opened his mouth, and beginning at this Scripture, preached Jesus to him. ³⁶ Now as they went down the road, they came to some water. And the eunuch said, "See, here is water. What hinders me from being baptized?"

³⁷ Then Philip said, "If you believe with all your heart, you may."

And he answered and said, "I believe that Jesus Christ is the Son of God."

³⁸ So he commanded the chariot to stand still. And both Philip and the eunuch went down into the water, and he baptized him. ³⁹ Now when they came up out of the water, the Spirit of the Lord caught Philip away, so that the eunuch saw him no more; and he went on his way rejoicing. ⁴⁰ But Philip was found at Azotus. And passing through, he preached in all the cities till he came to Caesarea.

EXPLORATION

1. What examples of the Holy Spirit's leading do you see in this story?

2. Why did God ask Philip to leave his preaching and go down a desert road?

3. What was significant about the person Philip encountered on the road?

4. How did Philip handle the opportunity that God gave him?

5. What problem did the man have whom Philip encountered?

6. What was the result of Philip's obedience to God?

INSPIRATION

You have the same Spirit working with you that Philip did. Some of you don't believe me. You're still cautious. I can hear you mumbling under your breath as you read, "Philip had something I don't. I've never heard an angel's voice." To which I counter, "How do you know Philip did?"

We assume he did. We've been taught he did. The flannelboard figures say he did. An angel puts his trumpet in Philip's ear and blares the announcement, and Philip has no choice. Flashing lights and fluttering wings are nothing to deny. The deacon had to go. But could our assumption be wrong? Could it be that the angel's voice was every bit as miraculous as the one you and I hear?

You've heard the voice whispering your name, haven't you? You've felt the nudge to go and sensed the urge to speak. Hasn't it occurred to you? . . .

You notice the fellow on the other side of the church auditorium. He looks a bit out of place, what with his strange clothing and all. You learn that he is from Africa, in town on business. The next Sunday he is back. And the third Sunday he is present. You introduce yourself. He tells you how he is fascinated by the faith and how he wants to learn more. Rather than offer to teach him, you simply urge him to read the Bible.

Later in the week, you regret not being more direct. You call the office where he is consulting and learn that he is leaving today for home. You know in your heart you can't let him leave. So you rush to the airport and find him awaiting his flight, with a Bible open on his lap.

"Do you understand what you are reading?" you inquire. "How can I, unless someone explains it to me?"

And so you, like Philip, explain. And he, like the Ethiopian, believes. Baptism is requested and baptism is offered. He catches a later flight and you catch a glimpse of what it means to be led by the Spirit.

Were there lights? You just lit one. Were there voices? You just were one. Was there a miracle? You just witnessed one. Who knows? If the Bible were being written today, that might be your name in the eighth chapter of Acts. (From *When God Whispers Your Name* by Max Lucado.)

REACTION

7. In what ways does God's Spirit lead us?

8. Why is it important to be sensitive to the Holy Spirit?

9. How can you learn to recognize God's voice?

10. When have you felt the Holy Spirit nudging you? What did you do?

11. What tends to hold you back from obeying that nudging?

12. What is the potential danger in ignoring the Spirit's leading?

LIFE LESSONS

Is there anyone you are not willing to tell about Jesus? Is there any place you are not willing to take the good news? Ask God to give you the same kind of willingness, attentiveness, and courage that you see in Philip. Let him direct you where he wants you to go.

DEVOTION

Father, too many times we fail to hear you speaking to us. Remind us to be quiet before you so that we can hear your voice. May we make decisions based on your leading, not according to our goals and desires. But most of all, Father, help us to cherish the gift of your Spirit.

JOURNALING

What can you do to listen to the Spirit's guidance today? How ready are you to cooperate if God speaks into your life?

_____

_____

_____

_____

_____

_____

FOR FURTHER READING

To complete the book of Acts during this twelve-part study, read Acts 8:1–40. For more Bible passages about the Holy Spirit's leading, see Luke 4:18; John 6:63; 14:26; 16:13; Romans 8:5, 26–27; Galatians 5:25; and 2 Peter 1:21.

GOD'S SAVING POWER

As he neared Damascus on his journey, suddenly a light from heaven flashed around him. He fell to the ground and heard a voice say to him, "Saul, Saul, why do you persecute me?"
ACTS 9:3–4

REFLECTION

God is the great "interrupter." At times he seems to sneak up in our lives, while at other times he intrudes into our plans. God chooses the approach and knows how to get our attention. No matter what road we may find ourselves on, God's power is more than enough to turn us around. Think of a time you have seen God's power revealed in the life of a friend, or perhaps in your own life. What happened to that person? How was God's power evident?

SITUATION

After Stephen's death, a Pharisee named Saul went on a rampage of persecution against the followers of Christ. When they fled from Jerusalem, Saul went on the road after them. He heard there was a large group in Damascus, so he obtained permission to travel there with an armed company to capture the believers and bring them back to Jerusalem for trial, imprisonment, and probably death. But something happened on the way there that stopped Paul in his tracks.

OBSERVATION

Read Acts 9:1–20 from the New International Version or the New King James Version.

NEW INTERNATIONAL VERSION
[1] Meanwhile, Saul was still breathing out murderous threats against the Lord's disciples. He went to the high priest [2] and asked him for letters to

the synagogues in Damascus, so that if he found any there who belonged to the Way, whether men or women, he might take them as prisoners to Jerusalem. [3] As he neared Damascus on his journey, suddenly a light from heaven flashed around him. [4] He fell to the ground and heard a voice say to him, "Saul, Saul, why do you persecute me?"

[5] "Who are you, Lord?" Saul asked.

"I am Jesus, whom you are persecuting," he replied. [6] "Now get up and go into the city, and you will be told what you must do."

[7] The men traveling with Saul stood there speechless; they heard the sound but did not see anyone. [8] Saul got up from the ground, but when he opened his eyes he could see nothing. So they led him by the hand into Damascus. [9] For three days he was blind, and did not eat or drink anything.

[10] In Damascus there was a disciple named Ananias. The Lord called to him in a vision, "Ananias!"

"Yes, Lord," he answered.

[11] The Lord told him, "Go to the house of Judas on Straight Street and ask for a man from Tarsus named Saul, for he is praying. [12] In a vision he has seen a man named Ananias come and place his hands on him to restore his sight."

[13] "Lord," Ananias answered, "I have heard many reports about this man and all the harm he has done to your holy people in Jerusalem. [14] And he has come here with authority from the chief priests to arrest all who call on your name."

[15] But the Lord said to Ananias, "Go! This man is my chosen instrument to proclaim my name to the Gentiles and their kings and to the people of Israel. [16] I will show him how much he must suffer for my name."

[17] Then Ananias went to the house and entered it. Placing his hands on Saul, he said, "Brother Saul, the Lord—Jesus, who appeared to you on the road as you were coming here—has sent me so that you may see again and be filled with the Holy Spirit." [18] Immediately, something like scales fell from Saul's eyes, and he could see again. He got up and was baptized, [19] and after taking some food, he regained his strength.

Saul spent several days with the disciples in Damascus. [20] At once he began to preach in the synagogues that Jesus is the Son of God.

New King James Version

[1] Then Saul, still breathing threats and murder against the disciples of the Lord, went to the high priest [2] and asked letters from him to the synagogues of Damascus, so that if he found any who were of the Way, whether men or women, he might bring them bound to Jerusalem.

[3] As he journeyed he came near Damascus, and suddenly a light shone around him from heaven. [4] Then he fell to the ground, and heard a voice saying to him, "Saul, Saul, why are you persecuting Me?"

[5] And he said, "Who are You, Lord?"

Then the Lord said, "I am Jesus, whom you are persecuting. It is hard for you to kick against the goads."

[6] So he, trembling and astonished, said, "Lord, what do You want me to do?"

Then the Lord said to him, "Arise and go into the city, and you will be told what you must do."

[7] And the men who journeyed with him stood speechless, hearing a voice but seeing no one. [8] Then Saul arose from the ground, and when his eyes were opened he saw no one. But they led him by the hand and brought him into Damascus. [9] And he was three days without sight, and neither ate nor drank.

[10] Now there was a certain disciple at Damascus named Ananias; and to him the Lord said in a vision, "Ananias."

And he said, "Here I am, Lord."

[11] So the Lord said to him, "Arise and go to the street called Straight, and inquire at the house of Judas for one called Saul of Tarsus, for behold, he is praying. [12] And in a vision he has seen a man named Ananias coming in and putting his hand on him, so that he might receive his sight."

[13] Then Ananias answered, "Lord, I have heard from many about this man, how much harm he has done to Your saints in Jerusalem. [14] And here he has authority from the chief priests to bind all who call on Your name."

[15] But the Lord said to him, "Go, for he is a chosen vessel of Mine to bear My name before Gentiles, kings, and the children of Israel. [16] For I will show him how many things he must suffer for My name's sake."

[17] And Ananias went his way and entered the house; and laying his hands on him he said, "Brother Saul, the Lord Jesus, who appeared to you on the road as you came, has sent me that you may receive your sight and be filled with the Holy Spirit." [18] Immediately there fell from his eyes something like scales, and he received his sight at once; and he arose and was baptized.

[19] So when he had received food, he was strengthened. Then Saul spent some days with the disciples at Damascus.

[20] Immediately he preached the Christ in the synagogues, that He is the Son of God.

EXPLORATION

1. How would you describe Saul before his encounter with Christ?

2. What did the voice from heaven tell Saul about his past and his future?

3. How long did Saul have to wait for further instructions from the Lord?

4. What doubts did Ananias express to God about Saul?

_____

_____

_____

_____

5. How did Ananias minister to Saul?

_____

_____

_____

6. How was God's power revealed in Saul's life?

_____

_____

_____

_____

INSPIRATION

Before he encountered Christ, Paul had been somewhat of a hero among the Pharisees . . . Blue-blooded and wild-eyed, this young zealot was hell-bent on keeping the kingdom pure—and that meant keeping the Christians out. He marched through the countryside like a general demanding that backslidden Jews salute the flag of the motherland or kiss their family and hopes good-bye.

All this came to a halt, however, on the shoulder of a highway . . . That's when someone slammed on the stadium lights, and he heard the voice.

When he found out whose voice it was, his jaw hit the ground, and his body followed. He braced himself for the worst. He knew it was all over. . . . He prayed that death would be quick and painless.

But all he got was silence and the first of a lifetime of surprises.

He ended up bewildered and befuddled in a borrowed bedroom. God left him there a few days with scales on his eyes so thick that the only direction he could look was inside himself. And he didn't like what he saw. He saw himself for what he really was—to use his own words, the worst of sinners. . . . Alone in the room with his sins on his conscience and blood on his hands, he asked to be cleansed. The legalist Saul was buried, and the liberator Paul was born. He was never the same afterward. And neither was the world.

The message is gripping: Show a man his failures without Jesus, and the result will be found in the roadside gutter. Give a man religion without reminding him of his filth, and the result will be arrogance in a three-piece suit. But get the two in the same heart—get sin to meet Savior and Savior to meet sin—and the result just might be another Pharisee turned preacher who sets the world on fire. (From *The Applause of Heaven* by Max Lucado.)

REACTION

7. Which person do you identify with the most: Saul, his companions, or Ananias? Why?

_____

_____

_____

8. What does this passage teach you about God? What does it teach you about people?

_____

_____

_____

9. What was your conversion experience like? Why is it helpful to share your story with others?

_____

_____

_____

10. What are some of the ways you feel God has used you to minister to unbelievers?

_____

_____

_____

_____

_____

11. When was a time that God used you to minister to someone else? What did you do?

_____

_____

_____

_____

_____

12. How will you minister to someone who has not yet experienced God's saving power?

_____

_____

_____

_____

_____

LIFE LESSONS

Life can be a stunning mixture of "Saul" experiences and "Ananias" opportunities. Sometimes we're the target, but sometimes we're the arrow. We are served, and we serve. Because we are first loved and saved, we get wonderful chances to participate in the miracle of other people's life change. On this side of eternity, we're never far from attitudes and sin that cause God to treat us like Saul on the road to Damascus, nor far from moments when God calls us to step into Ananias's sandals and walk into someone else's life.

DEVOTION

Father, when we think of what you have done for us, we can feel only humble gratitude. We can never thank you enough for sacrificing your Son to save us. You rescued us from an eternity of suffering and offered us everlasting joy. We praise you, Father, for displaying your saving power in us.

JOURNALING

What will you do today to thank God for saving you? Who could be your human sounding board for God's blessings in your life?

FOR FURTHER READING

To complete the book of Acts during this twelve-part study, read Acts 9:1–43. For more Bible passages about God's power to save, read Psalm 68:20; Daniel 3:17; Zephaniah 3:17; John 3:16–21; 6:44; Acts 22:14–16; Romans 10:9–13; and Hebrews 7:25.

UNITY AMONG BELIEVERS

Then Peter opened his mouth and said: "In truth I perceive that God shows no partiality. But in every nation whoever fears Him and works righteousness is accepted by Him."

ACTS 10:34–35 NKJV

REFLECTION

We know the church should be a place of harmony in which the people focus on worshipping and honoring God. But all too often church groups fall into the "we/them" trap of discord. The early church, made up of Jewish believers, also had these struggles. God wanted to expand the boundaries to the Gentiles, but they weren't quite ready for that. Think about your own church body. Is it a place of unity? Why or why not? How do you think "outsiders" feel when they visit?

SITUATION

One of the first non-Jews to embrace the gospel was Cornelius, a Roman centurion stationed at Palestinian Caesarea. God gave separate visions to Cornelius and Peter to set the stage for their meeting and to show Peter that Gentiles were included in God's plan—a radical idea. Peter was waiting for Cornelius's invitation. He did not know who waited for him in the Gentile's house, but he was under orders to be there and offer whoever would listen the message of salvation.

OBSERVATION

Read Acts 10:24–35 from the New International
Version or the New King James Version.

New International Version

24 The following day he arrived in Caesarea. Cornelius was expecting them and had called together his relatives and close friends. 25 As Peter entered

the house, Cornelius met him and fell at his feet in reverence. [26] But Peter made him get up. "Stand up," he said, "I am only a man myself."

[27] While talking with him, Peter went inside and found a large gathering of people. [28] He said to them: "You are well aware that it is against our law for a Jew to associate with or visit a Gentile. But God has shown me that I should not call anyone impure or unclean. [29] So when I was sent for, I came without raising any objection. May I ask why you sent for me?"

[30] Cornelius answered: "Three days ago I was in my house praying at this hour, at three in the afternoon. Suddenly a man in shining clothes stood before me [31] and said, 'Cornelius, God has heard your prayer and remembered your gifts to the poor. [32] Send to Joppa for Simon who is called Peter. He is a guest in the home of Simon the tanner, who lives by the sea.' [33] So I sent for you immediately, and it was good of you to come. Now we are all here in the presence of God to listen to everything the Lord has commanded you to tell us."

[34] Then Peter began to speak: "I now realize how true it is that God does not show favoritism [35] but accepts from every nation the one who fears him and does what is right."

NEW KING JAMES VERSION

[24] And the following day they entered Caesarea. Now Cornelius was waiting for them, and had called together his relatives and close friends. [25] As Peter was coming in, Cornelius met him and fell down at his feet and worshiped him. [26] But Peter lifted him up, saying, "Stand up; I myself am also a man." [27] And as he talked with him, he went in and found many who had come together. [28] Then he said to them, "You know how unlawful it is for a Jewish man to keep company with or go to one of another nation. But God has shown me that I should not call any man common or unclean. [29] Therefore I came without objection as soon as I was sent for. I ask, then, for what reason have you sent for me?"

[30] So Cornelius said, "Four days ago I was fasting until this hour; and at the ninth hour I prayed in my house, and behold, a man stood before me in bright clothing, [31] and said, 'Cornelius, your prayer has been heard, and

your alms are remembered in the sight of God. [32] Send therefore to Joppa and call Simon here, whose surname is Peter. He is lodging in the house of Simon, a tanner, by the sea. When he comes, he will speak to you.' [33] So I sent to you immediately, and you have done well to come. Now therefore, we are all present before God, to hear all the things commanded you by God."

[34] Then Peter opened his mouth and said: "In truth I perceive that God shows no partiality. [35] But in every nation whoever fears Him and works righteousness is accepted by Him."

EXPLORATION

1. How did Cornelius prepare for his meeting with Peter?

_____

_____

_____

2. Why was divine intervention necessary to bring Peter and Cornelius together?

_____

_____

_____

3. How did Peter demonstrate obedience to God in spite of his misgivings about associating with non-Jews?

_____

_____

_____

4. What did the angel say to Cornelius? What does this reveal about Cornelius's character?

_____

_____

_____

5. What did Cornelius want from Peter?

---

6. What lesson did God teach Peter through this meeting?

INSPIRATION

Peter was doing his best to pray with a growling stomach. "He became very hungry and wanted to eat; but while they made ready, he fell into a trance and saw heaven opened and an object like a great sheet bound at the four corners, descending to him and let down to the earth. In it were all kinds of four-footed animals of the earth, wild beasts, creeping things, and birds of the air. And a voice came to him, 'Rise, Peter; kill and eat'" (Acts 10:10–13 NKJV).

The sheet contained enough unkosher food to uncurl the payos of any Hasidic Jew. Peter absolutely and resolutely refused. "Not so, Lord! For I have never eaten anything common or unclean" (verse 14 NKJV).

But God wasn't kidding about this. He three-peated the vision, leaving poor Peter in a quandary. Peter was pondering the pigs in the blanket when he heard a knock at the door. At the sound of the knock, he heard the call of God's Spirit in his heart. "Behold, three men are seeking you. Arise therefore, go down and go with them, doubting nothing; for I have sent them" (verses 19–20 NKJV).

"Doubting nothing" can also be translated "make no distinction" or "indulge in no prejudice" or "discard all partiality." This was a huge moment for Peter. . . .

Peter told Cornelius about Jesus and the gospel, and before Peter could issue an invitation, the presence of the Spirit was among them, and they were replicating Pentecost—speaking in tongues and glorifying God. Peter offered to baptize Cornelius and his friends. They accepted. They offered him a bed. Peter accepted. By the end of the visit, he was making his own ham sandwiches.

And us? We are still pondering verse 28: "God has shown me that he doesn't think anyone is unclean or unfit" (NKJV). . . .

God calls us to change the way we look at people. Not to see them as Gentiles or Jews, insiders or outsiders, liberals or conservatives. . . . Let's view people differently; let's view them as we do ourselves. (From *Outlive Your Life* by Max Lucado.)

REACTION

7. What differences divide believers today?

_____

_____

_____

8. What issues do you think Christians should not fight over? What issues are worth discussing?

_____

_____

_____

9. What can you do to build a sense of unity in the church?

_____

_____

_____

10. Why is a lack of unity harmful to the church?

_____

_____

_____

11. How can believers remain unified when disagreements arise?

_____

_____

_____

_____

_____

_____

12. How can you help your Christian brothers and sisters focus on the common ground you share?

_____

_____

_____

_____

_____

LIFE LESSONS

For followers of Jesus today, the issue of unity boils down to how we welcome people into our fellowship. Are we quick to give forceful reasons why they shouldn't want to join us? Or are we eager to invite them to follow Jesus with us as the Lord works out change in each of our lives? Peter had a message to deliver, but his presence among the Gentiles delivered a powerful illustration that his message was true. Let your presence do the same.

DEVOTION

Father, your heart must break when you see selfishness, competition, and discord in your church. Help us to take our eyes off ourselves so we can focus on the common ground we share in you. Father, strengthen your church by filling us with your love.

JOURNALING

If you have contributed to any division in your church, what can you do to make things right?

_____

_____

_____

_____

_____

_____

_____

_____

_____

_____

_____

_____

_____

_____

_____

_____

_____

_____

_____

FOR FURTHER READING

To complete the book of Acts during this twelve-part study, read Acts 10:1–13:52. For more Bible passages about Christian unity, read 2 Chronicles 30:12; Psalm 133:1; John 17:23; Romans 15:5; Ephesians 4:3–13; Philippians 2:1; and Colossians 2:2; 3:14.

LESSON NINE

GOD'S GRACE

"We believe it is through the grace of our
Lord Jesus that we are saved."
ACTS 15:11

REFLECTION

One of the ways we resist change is by creating traditions. Thoughtful traditions bring stability to life—but they can also create a rigid environment where desperately needed change cannot occur. What is one of your favorite religious traditions? Why?

SITUATION

The Gentiles were turning to Christ by the scores, and it was clear they would soon outnumber the Jewish believers in the church. For some of these early Jewish Christians, the situation was getting out of hand. One way for them to cope with the situation was to insist that everyone had to accept the rules and culture of Judaism as part of the requirement before their faith in Christ would be recognized. But Paul and Barnabas insisted that such added regulations only complicated and undermined the gospel of Jesus Christ. Clearly, the stakes were high. So the church leaders in Jerusalem decided to bring the matter to an official decision.

OBSERVATION

Read Acts 15:1–11 from the New International Version or the New King James Version.

NEW INTERNATIONAL VERSION

[1] Certain people came down from Judea to Antioch and were teaching the believers: "Unless you are circumcised, according to the custom taught by Moses, you cannot be saved." [2] This brought Paul and Barnabas into sharp

dispute and debate with them. So Paul and Barnabas were appointed, along with some other believers, to go up to Jerusalem to see the apostles and elders about this question. ³ The church sent them on their way, and as they traveled through Phoenicia and Samaria, they told how the Gentiles had been converted. This news made all the believers very glad. ⁴ When they came to Jerusalem, they were welcomed by the church and the apostles and elders, to whom they reported everything God had done through them.

⁵ Then some of the believers who belonged to the party of the Pharisees stood up and said, "The Gentiles must be circumcised and required to keep the law of Moses."

⁶ The apostles and elders met to consider this question. ⁷ After much discussion, Peter got up and addressed them: "Brothers, you know that some time ago God made a choice among you that the Gentiles might hear from my lips the message of the gospel and believe. ⁸ God, who knows the heart, showed that he accepted them by giving the Holy Spirit to them, just as he did to us. ⁹ He did not discriminate between us and them, for he purified their hearts by faith. ¹⁰ Now then, why do you try to test God by putting on the necks of Gentiles a yoke that neither we nor our ancestors have been able to bear? ¹¹ No! We believe it is through the grace of our Lord Jesus that we are saved, just as they are."

New King James Version

¹ And certain men came down from Judea and taught the brethren, "Unless you are circumcised according to the custom of Moses, you cannot be saved." ² Therefore, when Paul and Barnabas had no small dissension and dispute with them, they determined that Paul and Barnabas and certain others of them should go up to Jerusalem, to the apostles and elders, about this question.

³ So, being sent on their way by the church, they passed through Phoenicia and Samaria, describing the conversion of the Gentiles; and they caused great joy to all the brethren. ⁴ And when they had come to Jerusalem, they were received by the church and the apostles and the elders; and they reported all things that God had done with them. ⁵ But

some of the sect of the Pharisees who believed rose up, saying, "It is necessary to circumcise them, and to command them to keep the law of Moses."

⁶ Now the apostles and elders came together to consider this matter. ⁷ And when there had been much dispute, Peter rose up and said to them: "Men and brethren, you know that a good while ago God chose among us, that by my mouth the Gentiles should hear the word of the gospel and believe. ⁸ So God, who knows the heart, acknowledged them by giving them the Holy Spirit, just as He did to us, ⁹ and made no distinction between us and them, purifying their hearts by faith. ¹⁰ Now therefore, why do you test God by putting a yoke on the neck of the disciples which neither our fathers nor we were able to bear? ¹¹ But we believe that through the grace of the Lord Jesus Christ we shall be saved in the same manner as they."

EXPLORATION

1. What sparked controversy in the Gentile churches where Paul and Barnabas were serving?

_____

_____

_____

2. How did the Gentile believers decide to resolve the problem?

_____

_____

_____

3. What requirements were the Jewish believers trying to impose on the Gentile believers?

_____

_____

_____

4. How did Peter say that God had shown his acceptance of the Gentile believers?

_____

_____

_____

5. Why did Peter accuse some of these Jewish believers of testing God?

_____

_____

_____

6. What final statement did Peter make to the council about salvation?

_____

_____

_____

INSPIRATION

God is not the God of confusion, and wherever he sees sincere seekers with confused hearts, you can bet your sweet December that he will do whatever it takes to help them see his will. . . . His plan hasn't changed. Jesus still speaks to believers through believers. "The whole body depends on Christ, and all the parts of the body are joined and held together. Each part does its own work to make the whole body grow and be strong with love" (Ephesians 4:16 NCV).

While I was driving to my office this morning, my eye saw a traffic light. The sensors within my eye perceived that the color of the light was red. My brain checked my memory bank and announced the meaning of a red light to my right foot. My right foot responded by leaving the accelerator and pressing the brake.

Now, what if my body hadn't functioned properly? What if my eye had decided not to be a part of the body because the nose had hurt its feelings? Or what if the foot was tired of being bossed around and decided to press the gas pedal instead of the brake? Or what if the right foot was in pain, but too proud to tell the left foot, so the left foot didn't know to step in and help? In all instances, a wreck would occur.

God has given each part of the body of Christ an assignment. One way God reveals his will to you is through the church. He speaks to one member of his body through another member. It could happen in a Bible class, a small group, during communion, or during dessert. God has as many methods as he has people. (From *The Great House of God* by Max Lucado.)

REACTION

7. How does the gracious attitude of Paul, Barnabas, and Peter challenge you?

_____

_____

_____

8. What does it mean to extend God's grace to others?

_____

_____

_____

9. Why do you think it is difficult for some people to receive God's acceptance by grace?

_____

_____

_____

10. What traditions or practices have some Christians added to the gospel?

_____

_____

_____

11. How can you determine whether the requirements for faith taught in your church has been established by God or by people?

_____

_____

_____

_____

12. How can you guard against expecting more of new Christians than God expects?

_____

_____

_____

_____

LIFE LESSONS

Some differences between Christians boil down to preferences. The early believers had to discover a way to settle these differences so that truthful and godly standards could remain but insignificant alternatives could be accepted. How do you react to Christians whose worship style is different from your own? Remember God's gift of eternal life is free and for everybody, regardless of their color, race, or worship preference. Have the same gracious attitude toward others that Jesus had.

DEVOTION

Father, forgive us for the times we have insulted you by trying to earn your acceptance. And forgive us for putting heavy burdens on others who want to know you. We know that you save people not because of what they have done but because of your amazing grace.

JOURNALING

How does this passage deepen your understanding of God's grace? What difference should this make in your daily life?

_____

_____

_____

_____

_____

_____

_____

_____

_____

_____

_____

_____

_____

_____

_____

_____

_____

_____

_____

_____

_____

FOR FURTHER READING

To complete the book of Acts during this twelve-part study, read Acts 14:1–16:40. For more Bible passages about grace, read Romans 3:23–24; 2 Corinthians 12:9; Galatians 2:15–21; Ephesians 2:4–9; 2 Thessalonians 2:16–17; 1 Timothy 1:14; Titus 3:4–7; and Hebrews 12:15.

PRESENTING THE GOSPEL

They took him and brought him to the Areopagus, saying,
"May we know what this new doctrine is of which you speak?
For you are bringing some strange things to our ears."
ACTS 17:19–20 NKJV

REFLECTION

Most of us instinctively avoid the direct approach when it comes to witnessing. Some of us can manage this approach without offending, but most of us settle for something a bit more subtle. We want to connect with people and share with a reasonable expectation of gaining a hearing. What do you think attracts people to Christianity? What turns people away?

SITUATION

By this point in Paul's missionary career, God was already using him greatly to start new churches. Paul's travels eventually led him to Athens, the philosophical capital of the world, where he hoped to gain a hearing among the intellectuals. As he walked through the city's market, he made an observation that stunned him. His opening to the philosophers became obvious: he would start with the history, culture, and traditions of his audience.

OBSERVATION

Read Acts 17:16–31 from the New International
Version or the New King James Version.

NEW INTERNATIONAL VERSION
[16] While Paul was waiting for them in Athens, he was greatly distressed to see that the city was full of idols. [17] So he reasoned in the synagogue with

both Jews and God-fearing Greeks, as well as in the marketplace day by day with those who happened to be there. [18] A group of Epicurean and Stoic philosophers began to debate with him. Some of them asked, "What is this babbler trying to say?" Others remarked, "He seems to be advocating foreign gods." They said this because Paul was preaching the good news about Jesus and the resurrection. [19] Then they took him and brought him to a meeting of the Areopagus, where they said to him, "May we know what this new teaching is that you are presenting? [20] You are bringing some strange ideas to our ears, and we would like to know what they mean." [21] (All the Athenians and the foreigners who lived there spent their time doing nothing but talking about and listening to the latest ideas.)

[22] Paul then stood up in the meeting of the Areopagus and said: "People of Athens! I see that in every way you are very religious. [23] For as I walked around and looked carefully at your objects of worship, I even found an altar with this inscription: TO AN UNKNOWN GOD. So you are ignorant of the very thing you worship—and this is what I am going to proclaim to you.

[24] "The God who made the world and everything in it is the Lord of heaven and earth and does not live in temples built by human hands. [25] And he is not served by human hands, as if he needed anything. Rather, he himself gives everyone life and breath and everything else. [26] From one man he made all the nations, that they should inhabit the whole earth; and he marked out their appointed times in history and the boundaries of their lands. [27] God did this so that they would seek him and perhaps reach out for him and find him, though he is not far from any one of us. [28] 'For in him we live and move and have our being.' As some of your own poets have said, 'We are his offspring.'

[29] "Therefore since we are God's offspring, we should not think that the divine being is like gold or silver or stone—an image made by human design and skill. [30] In the past God overlooked such ignorance, but now he commands all people everywhere to repent. [31] For he has set a day when he will judge the world with justice by the man he has appointed. He has given proof of this to everyone by raising him from the dead."

NEW KING JAMES VERSION

[16] Now while Paul waited for them at Athens, his spirit was provoked within him when he saw that the city was given over to idols. [17] Therefore he reasoned in the synagogue with the Jews and with the Gentile worshipers, and in the marketplace daily with those who happened to be there. [18] Then certain Epicurean and Stoic philosophers encountered him. And some said, "What does this babbler want to say?"

Others said, "He seems to be a proclaimer of foreign gods," because he preached to them Jesus and the resurrection.

[19] And they took him and brought him to the Areopagus, saying, "May we know what this new doctrine is of which you speak? [20] For you are bringing some strange things to our ears. Therefore we want to know what these things mean." [21] For all the Athenians and the foreigners who were there spent their time in nothing else but either to tell or to hear some new thing.

[22] Then Paul stood in the midst of the Areopagus and said, "Men of Athens, I perceive that in all things you are very religious; [23] for as I was passing through and considering the objects of your worship, I even found an altar with this inscription:

TO THE UNKNOWN GOD.

Therefore, the One whom you worship without knowing, Him I proclaim to you: [24] "God, who made the world and everything in it, since He is Lord of heaven and earth, does not dwell in temples made with hands. [25] Nor is He worshiped with men's hands, as though He needed anything, since He gives to all life, breath, and all things. [26] And He has made from one blood every nation of men to dwell on all the face of the earth, and has determined their preappointed times and the boundaries of their dwellings, [27] so that they should seek the Lord, in the hope that they might grope for Him and find Him, though He is not far from each one of us; [28] for in Him we live and move and have our being, as also some of your own poets have said, 'For we are also His offspring.' [29] Therefore, since we are the offspring of God, we ought not to think that the Divine Nature is like gold or silver or stone, something shaped by art and man's devising. [30] Truly, these times of ignorance God overlooked, but now commands all men everywhere to repent, [31] because He has appointed a day on which He will judge the world in righteousness by the Man whom He has ordained. He has given assurance of this to all by raising Him from the dead."

EXPLORATION

1. What motivated Paul to preach the gospel in Athens?

2. How did the people in Athens initially respond to Paul's message?

3. How did Paul use his knowledge of the culture to present his case to the council?

4. How did Paul explain that the true God is different from other gods?

5. What warning did Paul give to the people of Athens?

_____

_____

_____

6. What proof did Paul say God has given about the Day of Judgment?

_____

_____

_____

INSPIRATION

It's not God's plan for your heart to roam as a Bedouin. God wants you to move in out of the cold and live . . . with him. Under his roof there is space available. At his table a plate is set. In his living room a wingback chair is reserved just for you. And he'd like you to take up residence in his house. Why would he want you to share his home?

Simple, he's your Father.

You were intended to live in your Father's house. Any place less than his is insufficient. Any place far from his is dangerous. Only the home built for your heart can protect your heart. And your Father wants you to dwell _in_ him.

No, you didn't misread the sentence and I didn't miswrite it. Your Father doesn't ask you to live _with_ him, he asks you to live _in_ him. As Paul wrote, "For in him we live and move and have our being" (Acts 17:28).

Don't think you are separated from God, he at the top end of a great ladder, you at the other. Dismiss any thought that God is on Venus while you are on earth. Since God is Spirit (see John 4:23), he is next to you: God himself is our wall. And God himself is our foundation. . . .

For many this is a new thought. We think of God as a deity to discuss, not a place to dwell. We think of God as a mysterious miracle worker, not a house to live in. We think of God as a creator to call on, not a home to reside in. But our Father wants to be much more. He wants to be the one in whom "we live and move and have our being" (Acts 17:28).

Heaven knows no difference between Sunday morning and Wednesday afternoon. God longs to speak as clearly in the workplace as he does in the sanctuary. He longs to be worshipped when we sit at the dinner table and not just when we come to his communion table. You may go days without thinking of him, but there's not a moment when he's not thinking of you. (From *The Great House of God* by Max Lucado.)

REACTION

7. How does the fact that God dwells in you give you courage to speak out about him?

_____

_____

_____

_____

_____

8. What can you model from Paul's methods when you share your faith with others?

_____

_____

_____

_____

_____

9. What is the danger in changing your approach and presentation to fit your audience?

_____

_____

_____

_____

_____

10. What points should you include while sharing the gospel with non-Christians?

_____

_____

_____

_____

11. What happens when Christians assume everyone has the same perspective and background? List several cultural factors you think Christians should consider in their evangelistic efforts.

_____

_____

_____

_____

12. What are some ways you can share the gospel with co-workers or friends?

_____

_____

_____

_____

LIFE LESSONS

One of the great lessons we can take from Paul's experience in Athens has to do with his practice of observing people. He looked for clues to their life-quests. He knew that what people were involved in often revealed what they were looking for, even if they didn't realize it. Believers who become observant of people around them likewise discover all kinds of opportunities and open doors for sharing their faith. Meanwhile, a believer's life should also provoke questions such as, "Why are you so hopeful in your outlook?" (see 1 Peter 3:15).

DEVOTION

Father, we cannot communicate the truth of the gospel without your help. Take our fears and inadequacies and use them to advance your kingdom. Give us your heart for the lost, your compassion for the hurting, and your wisdom for the troubled. Speak through us to draw people to yourself.

JOURNALING

What is keeping you from effectively sharing your testimony with others? How can you begin to eliminate those hindrances?

FOR FURTHER READING

To complete the book of Acts during this twelve-part study, read Acts 17:1– 20:14. For more Bible passages about witnessing, read Acts 1:8; Romans 1:14–16; 15:15– 20; 1 Corinthians 1:17; 9:16–18; 1 Thessalonians 2:4–13; and 2 Timothy 4:2–5.

FACING PROBLEMS AND PAIN

*"And now, compelled by the Spirit, I am going to
Jerusalem, not knowing what will happen to me there.
I only know that in every city the Holy Spirit warns
me that prison and hardships are facing me."*
ACTS 20:22–23

REFLECTION

Pain, difficulty, and struggles always feel and look different when they invade our lives. The responses we expect from others seem harder for us to practice. If we haven't decided beforehand how we will view problems, they will dictate our responses. Think of a time when you have seen someone display joy or courage even in the midst of suffering. How do you think that person was able to be joyful or courageous?

SITUATION

As Paul's third missionary journey was winding down, he still had many objectives he wanted to accomplish, such as visiting Spain. Yet he became aware that his time for ministry was coming to an end. He was on the way to Jerusalem, and he expected that events there would lead him in a radical new direction. At one point, Paul gathered together the elders and leaders of the church in Ephesus, where he had served for many years, and gave them some parting words.

OBSERVATION

Read Acts 20:15–31 from the New International Version or the New King James Version.

New International Version

15 The next day we set sail from there and arrived off Chios. The day after that we crossed over to Samos, and on the following day arrived at Miletus. 16 Paul had decided to sail past Ephesus to avoid spending time in the

province of Asia, for he was in a hurry to reach Jerusalem, if possible, by the day of Pentecost.

[17] From Miletus, Paul sent to Ephesus for the elders of the church. [18] When they arrived, he said to them: "You know how I lived the whole time I was with you, from the first day I came into the province of Asia. [19] I served the Lord with great humility and with tears and in the midst of severe testing by the plots of my Jewish opponents. [20] You know that I have not hesitated to preach anything that would be helpful to you but have taught you publicly and from house to house. [21] I have declared to both Jews and Greeks that they must turn to God in repentance and have faith in our Lord Jesus.

[22] "And now, compelled by the Spirit, I am going to Jerusalem, not knowing what will happen to me there. [23] I only know that in every city the Holy Spirit warns me that prison and hardships are facing me. [24] However, I consider my life worth nothing to me; my only aim is to finish the race and complete the task the Lord Jesus has given me—the task of testifying to the good news of God's grace.

[25] "Now I know that none of you among whom I have gone about preaching the kingdom will ever see me again. [26] Therefore, I declare to you today that I am innocent of the blood of any of you. [27] For I have not hesitated to proclaim to you the whole will of God. [28] Keep watch over yourselves and all the flock of which the Holy Spirit has made you overseers. Be shepherds of the church of God, which he bought with his own blood. [29] I know that after I leave, savage wolves will come in among you and will not spare the flock. [30] Even from your own number men will arise and distort the truth in order to draw away disciples after them. [31] So be on your guard! Remember that for three years I never stopped warning each of you night and day with tears.

New King James Version

[15] We sailed from there, and the next day came opposite Chios. The following day we arrived at Samos and stayed at Trogyllium. The next day we came to Miletus. [16] For Paul had decided to sail past Ephesus, so that he would not have to spend time in Asia; for he was hurrying to be at Jerusalem, if possible, on the Day of Pentecost.

[17] From Miletus he sent to Ephesus and called for the elders of the church. [18] And when they had come to him, he said to them: "You know, from the first day that I came to Asia, in what manner I always lived among you, [19] serving the Lord with all humility, with many tears and trials which happened to me by the plotting of the Jews; [20] how I kept back nothing that was helpful, but proclaimed it to you, and taught you publicly and from house to house, [21] testifying to Jews, and also to Greeks, repentance toward God and faith toward our Lord Jesus Christ. [22] And see, now I go bound in the spirit to Jerusalem, not knowing the things that will happen to me there, [23] except that the Holy Spirit testifies in every city, saying that chains and tribulations await me. [24] But none of these things move me; nor do I count my life dear to myself, so that I may finish my race with joy, and the ministry which I received from the Lord Jesus, to testify to the gospel of the grace of God.

[25] "And indeed, now I know that you all, among whom I have gone preaching the kingdom of God, will see my face no more. [26] Therefore I testify to you this day that I am innocent of the blood of all men. [27] For I have not shunned to declare to you the whole counsel of God. [28] Therefore take heed to yourselves and to all the flock, among which the Holy Spirit has made you overseers, to shepherd the church of God which He purchased with His own blood. [29] For I know this, that after my departure savage wolves will come in among you, not sparing the flock. [30] Also from among yourselves men will rise up, speaking perverse things, to draw away the disciples after themselves. [31] Therefore watch, and remember that for three years I did not cease to warn everyone night and day with tears.

EXPLORATION

1. Why did Paul ask the church elders to meet him in Miletus?

2. How was Paul tested during his ministry in Asia?

3. How did the Holy Spirit work in Paul's life?

4. What was Paul's attitude toward the hardships he faced?

5. What was Paul's goal in life?

6. What were Paul's closing instructions to the elders?

INSPIRATION

As you think about hardships, how do you explain yours? The tension at home. The demands at work. The bills on your desk or the tumor in your body. You aren't taken hostage, but aren't you occasionally taken aback by God's silence? He knows what you are facing. How do we explain this?

Maybe God messed up. Cancer cells crept into your DNA when he wasn't looking. He was so occupied with the tornado in Kansas that he forgot the famine in Uganda. He tried to change the stubborn streak in your spouse but just couldn't get him to budge. Honestly. A bumbling Creator? An absent-minded Maker?

What evidence does Scripture provide to support such a view? What evidence does creation offer? Can't the Maker of heaven and earth handle bad traffic and prevent bad marriages? Of course he can. Then why doesn't he?

Perhaps he is mad. Have we so exhausted the mercy of God's bank account that every prayer bounces like a bad check? Did humanity cross the line millenniums ago, and now we're getting what we deserve? Such an argument carries a dash of merit. God does leave us to the consequences of our stupid decisions. Think of Egyptian soldiers in the Red Sea, Hebrews in Babylon, Peter weeping with the sound of a crowing rooster in his ears. Bang your head against the wall, and expect a headache.

God lets us endure the fruit of sin. But to label him peeved and impatient? To do so you need to scissor from your Bible some tender passages such as: "God is sheer mercy and grace; not easily angered, he's rich in love. He doesn't endlessly nag and scold, nor hold grudges forever. He doesn't treat us as our sins deserve, nor pay us back in full for our wrongs. As high as heaven is over the earth, so strong is his love to those who fear him" (Psalm 103:8–11 msg).

Don't blame suffering in the world on the anger of God. He's not mad; he didn't mess up. Follow our troubles to their headwaters, and you won't find an angry or befuddled God. But you will find a sovereign God.

Your pain has a purpose. Your problems, struggles, heartaches, and hassles cooperate toward one end—the glory of God. "Trust me in your times of trouble, and I will rescue you, and you will give me glory" (Psalm 50:15 NLT). Not an easy assignment to swallow. Not for you. Not for me. (From *It's Not About Me* by Max Lucado.)

REACTION

7. Why is it important to recognize that pain is inevitable?

8. How do some people make their problems worse?

9. How can the Holy Spirit help you through life's difficulties?

10. Why do people try to handle their pain and problems on their own?

11. What lessons has God taught you through the hardships you have endured?

_____

_____

_____

_____

_____

12. How does this passage challenge you to deal with your present problems?

_____

_____

_____

_____

_____

LIFE LESSONS

In his wisdom, God seldom lets us know what will happen and how bad it may be. He tells us to trust him with all the arrangements. Our tendencies may always drift toward self-pity and questions, but God's Spirit will draw us back toward the truth. Every day becomes a new opportunity to discover in just how many different ways "it isn't about us." Life is about God's purposes and plans.

DEVOTION

Father, you promised there would be faith and strength and hope to meet life's problems. Give that strength to those of us whose anxieties have buried our dreams, whose illnesses have hospitalized our hopes, and whose burdens are bigger than our shoulders.

JOURNALING

What burdens are weighing you down? How can you release those problems to God?

FOR FURTHER READING

To complete the book of Acts during this twelve-part study, read Acts 20:15–24:23. For more Bible passages about facing pain and problems, read Job 33:19–26; Psalm 34:19; Romans 5:3–4; 2 Corinthians 4:17–18; 2 Thessalonians 1:4–5; James 1:2–4; and 1 Peter 1:6–7; 4:12–16.

LIVING YOUR FAITH

After long abstinence from food, then Paul stood in the midst of them and said, "Men, you should have listened to me, and not have sailed from Crete and incurred this disaster and loss. And now I urge you to take heart, for there will be no loss of life among you."

ACTS 27: 21–22 NKJV

REFLECTION

Faith seems to shine out when we experience times that are challenging or disastrous. But we don't have to wait until something difficult occurs before we find out whether our faith is effective. What are some ways you have found to flex your faith muscles on ordinary days?

SITUATION

Paul had placed his life in God's hands. He had already faced death many times, and he fully expected to die in God's service in some way. His plans to visit Rome had taken a long detour but were finally coming to pass. But then disaster struck. He and his companions, along with their guards, were stuck on a ship in a life-threatening storm. As the storm raged on for fourteen days, Paul was able to share with sailors what it meant to live with God's hope.

OBSERVATION

*Read Acts 27:13–25 from the New International
Version or the New King James Version.*

NEW INTERNATIONAL VERSION

[13] When a gentle south wind began to blow, they saw their opportunity; so they weighed anchor and sailed along the shore of Crete. [14] Before very long, a wind of hurricane force, called the Northeaster, swept down from the island. [15] The ship was caught by the storm and could not head into the wind; so we gave way to it and were driven along. [16] As we passed to the

lee of a small island called Cauda, we were hardly able to make the life-boat secure, [17] so the men hoisted it aboard. Then they passed ropes under the ship itself to hold it together. Because they were afraid they would run aground on the sandbars of Syrtis, they lowered the sea anchor and let the ship be driven along. [18] We took such a violent battering from the storm that the next day they began to throw the cargo overboard. [19] On the third day, they threw the ship's tackle overboard with their own hands. [20] When neither sun nor stars appeared for many days and the storm continued raging, we finally gave up all hope of being saved.

[21] After they had gone a long time without food, Paul stood up before them and said: "Men, you should have taken my advice not to sail from Crete; then you would have spared yourselves this damage and loss. [22] But now I urge you to keep up your courage, because not one of you will be lost; only the ship will be destroyed. [23] Last night an angel of the God to whom I belong and whom I serve stood beside me [24] and said, 'Do not be afraid, Paul. You must stand trial before Caesar; and God has graciously given you the lives of all who sail with you.' [25] So keep up your courage, men, for I have faith in God that it will happen just as he told me.

New King James Version

[13] When the south wind blew softly, supposing that they had obtained their desire, putting out to sea, they sailed close by Crete. [14] But not long after, a tempestuous head wind arose, called Euroclydon. [15] So when the ship was caught, and could not head into the wind, we let her drive. [16] And running under the shelter of an island called Clauda, we secured the skiff with difficulty. [17] When they had taken it on board, they used cables to undergird the ship; and fearing lest they should run aground on the Syrtis Sands, they struck sail and so were driven. [18] And because we were exceedingly tempest-tossed, the next day they lightened the ship. [19] On the third day we threw the ship's tackle overboard with our own hands. [20] Now when neither sun nor stars appeared for many days, and no small tempest beat on us, all hope that we would be saved was finally given up.

²¹ But after long abstinence from food, then Paul stood in the midst of them and said, "Men, you should have listened to me, and not have sailed from Crete and incurred this disaster and loss. ²² And now I urge you to take heart, for there will be no loss of life among you, but only of the ship. ²³ For there stood by me this night an angel of the God to whom I belong and whom I serve, ²⁴ saying, 'Do not be afraid, Paul; you must be brought before Caesar; and indeed God has granted you all those who sail with you.' ²⁵ Therefore take heart, men, for I believe God that it will be just as it was told me.

EXPLORATION

1. What life-threatening situation did Paul face on his way to Rome?

_____

_____

_____

2. What steps did the sailors take to survive the storm?

_____

_____

_____

3. When did the people on board the ship lose hope of surviving?

_____

_____

_____

4. How did Paul demonstrate his faith in God in the midst of a seemingly hopeless situation?

_____

_____

_____

_____

5. Why did Paul reprimand the men on the boat?

_____

_____

_____

_____

6. How did Paul encourage everyone while warning them of the danger ahead?

_____

_____

_____

_____

INSPIRATION

The components of the perfect storm were gathering. A winter sea. A ferocious wind. A cumbersome boat. An impatient crew.

Individually these elements were manageable, but collectively they were formidable. So the crew did what they could. They hoisted the lifeboat aboard and frapped the vessel. They lowered the sea anchor, jettisoned cargo, and threw equipment overboard. But nothing worked.

Acts 27:20 reads like a death sentence: "Now when neither sun nor stars appeared for many days, and no small tempest beat on us, all hope that we would be saved was finally given up" (NKJV).

The perfect storm took its toll. It lasted for fourteen days! Fourteen hours would shake you. (Fourteen minutes would undo me!) But two weeks of sunless days and starless nights? Fourteen days of bouncing, climbing toward the heavens and plunging toward the sea. The ocean boomed, splashed, and rumbled. The sailors lost all appetite for food. They lost all reason for hope. They gave up. And when they gave up, Paul spoke up.

"But after long abstinence from food, then Paul stood in the midst of them and said, 'Men, you should have listened to me, and not have sailed from Crete and incurred this disaster and loss. And now I urge you to take heart, for there will be no loss of life among you, but only of the ship'" (verses 21–22 NKJV).

What a contrast. The mariners, who knew how to sail in storms, gave up hope. Paul, a Jewish preacher who presumably knew very little about sailing, became the courier of courage. What did he know that they didn't?

Better question, what did he say that you need to hear? Are you bouncing about in a northeaster? Like the sailors you've done all you can to survive: you've tightened the ship, lowered the anchor. You've consulted the bank, changed your diet, called the lawyers, called your supervisor, tightened your budget. You've gone for counseling, rehab, or therapy. Yet the sea churns with angry foam. Is fear coming at you from all sides? Then let God speak to you. Let God give you what he gave the sailors: perfect peace. (From *Anxious for Nothing* by Max Lucado.)

REACTION

7. Why was Paul able to maintain his confidence in God when the others had given up hope?

---

8. In what ways would you like to be more like Paul?

---

9. What does it mean to live out your faith in front of others?

---

10. What are some ways to remind yourself that others are watching the way you live?

_____

_____

_____

_____

11. What are some "perfect storms" that you have faced in your life?

_____

_____

_____

_____

12. What do you need to hear from God today in the midst of the trials you are experiencing?

_____

_____

_____

_____

LIFE LESSONS

The book of Acts doesn't really end here. The record ceases, but the acts of the disciples go on, down through the ages. Just as Jesus promised, the fragile group of men and women who gathered in Jerusalem were given power to become effective witnesses—sometimes even against their wishes. They left a legacy of faith for us to live out and pass on. They knew that no matter the circumstances in which they found themselves, God was always with them, following their every step. It was their role to run the race and keep the faith by sharing it with others. God likewise wants to work in us and through us even when the storms and shipwrecks of life come. What kinds of "acts of disciples" will your chapter in God's story include?

DEVOTION

Without you, Father, we know it is impossible to live righteously. So we ask you to come alongside us and give us the strength to live out what we believe. Help us to stand out as beacons of light for you in this dark and hurting world.

JOURNALING

How do you usually react when things go wrong in your life? What can you do differently in the future to demonstrate your faith in God?

FOR FURTHER READING

To complete the book of Acts during this twelve-part study, read Acts 24:24–28:31. For more Bible passages about living your faith, read Galatians 2:20; 1 Thessalonians 4:1–2; 1 Timothy 6:11–12; 2 Timothy 4:7; Titus 2:11–14; Hebrews 4:14; James 2:14–17; and 1 Peter 5:8–9.

LEADER'S GUIDE FOR SMALL GROUPS

Thank you for your willingness to lead a group through *Life Lessons from Acts*. The rewards of being a leader are different from those of participating, and we hope you find your own walk with Jesus deepened by this experience. During the twelve lessons in this study, you will guide your group through selected passages in Acts and explore the key themes of the book. There are several elements in this leader's guide that will help you as you structure your study and reflection time, so be sure to follow along and take advantage of each one.

BEFORE YOU BEGIN

Before your first meeting, make sure the group members have their own copy of the *Life Lessons from Acts* study guide so they can follow along and have their answers written out ahead of time. Alternately, you can hand out the guides at your first meeting and give the group some time to look over the material and ask any preliminary questions. Be sure to send a sheet around the room during that first meeting and have the members write down their name, phone number, and email address so you can keep in touch with them during the week.

There are several ways to structure the duration of the study. You can choose to cover each lesson individually for a total of twelve weeks of discussion, or you can combine two lessons together per week for a total of six weeks of discussion. You can also choose to have the group members read just the selected passages of Scripture given in each lesson, or they can cover the entire book of Acts by reading the material listed in the "For Further Reading" section at the end of each lesson. The following table illustrates these options:

Six-Week Format

Week	Lessons Covered	Simplified Reading	Expanded Reading
1	Jesus Changes Lives / We Are Witnesses	Acts 2:29–47; 3:1–16	Acts 1:1–4:37
2	A New Standard / Christ's Compassion	Acts 5:17–33; 6:1–15	Acts 5:1–6:15
3	Christ's Authority / Believing in Jesus	Acts 7:51–60; 8:26–40	Acts 7:1–8:40
4	Persistent Prayer / Trusting God	Acts 9:1–20; 10:24–35	Acts 9:1–13:52
5	God's Love for People / True Worship	Acts 15:1–11; 17:16–31	Acts 14:1–20:16
6	Christ's Sacrifice / Seeing Jesus	Acts 20:17–31; 27:13–25	Acts 20:17–28:31

Twelve-Week Format

Week	Lessons Covered	Simplified Reading	Expanded Reading
1	Jesus Changes Lives	Acts 2:29–47	Acts 1:1–2:47
2	We Are Witnesses	Acts 3:1–16	Acts 3:1–4:37
3	Tried and Tested	Acts 5:17–33	Acts 5:1–42
4	Getting Along with Others	Acts 6:1–15	Acts 6:1–15
5	Looking to Jesus	Acts 7:51–60	Acts 7:1–60
6	The Holy Spirit's Leading	Acts 8:26–40	Acts 8:1–40
7	God's Saving Power	Acts 9:1–20	Acts 9:1–43
8	Unity Among Believers	Acts 10:24–35	Acts 10:1–13:52
9	God's Grace	Acts 15:1–11	Acts 14:1–16:40
10	Presenting the Gospel	Acts 17:16–31	Acts 17:1–20:14
11	Facing Problems and Pain	Acts 20:15–31	Acts 20:15–24:23
12	Living Your Faith	Acts 27:13–25	Acts 24:24–28:31

Generally, the ideal size you will want for the group is between eight to ten people, which ensures everyone will have enough time to participate in discussions. If you have more people, you might want to break up the main group into smaller subgroups. Encourage those who show up at the first meeting to commit to attending the duration of the study, as this will help the group members get to know each other, create stability for the group, and help you know how to prepare each week.

Each of the lessons begins with a brief reflection that highlights the theme you will be discussing that week. As you begin your group time, have the group members briefly respond to the opening question to get them thinking about the topic at hand. Some people may want to tell a long story in response to one of these questions, but the goal is to keep the answers brief. Ideally, you want everyone in the group to get a chance to answer, so try to keep the responses to just a few minutes. If you have more talkative group members, say up front that everyone needs to limit his or her answer to two minutes.

Give the group members a chance to answer, but tell them to feel free to pass if they wish. With the rest of the study, it's generally not a good idea to have everyone answer every question—a free-flowing discussion is more desirable. But with the opening reflection question, you can go around the circle. Encourage shy people to share, but don't force them.

Before your first meeting, let the group members know how the lessons are broken down. During your group discussion time the members will be drawing on the answers they wrote to the Exploration and Reaction sections, so encourage them to always complete these ahead of time. Also, invite them to bring any questions and insights they uncovered while reading to your next meeting, especially if they had a breakthrough moment or if they didn't understand something they read.

WEEKLY PREPARATION

As the leader, there are a few things you should do to prepare for each meeting:

- *Read through the lesson.* This will help you to become familiar with the content and know how to structure the discussion times.
- *Decide which questions you want to discuss.* Depending on how you structure your group time, you may not be able to cover every question. So select the questions ahead of time that you absolutely want the group to explore.
- *Be familiar with the questions you want to discuss.* When the group meets you'll be watching the clock, so you want to make sure you are familiar with the Bible study questions you have selected. You can then spend time in the passage again when the group meets. In this way, you'll ensure you have the passage more deeply in your mind than your group members.
- *Pray for your group.* Pray for your group members throughout the week and ask God to lead them as they study his Word.
- *Bring extra supplies to your meeting.* The members should bring their own pens for writing notes, but it's a good idea to have extras available for those who forget. You may also want to bring paper and additional Bibles.

Note that in many cases there will not be one "right" answer to the question. Answers will vary, especially when the group members are being asked to share their personal experiences.

STRUCTURING THE DISCUSSION TIME

You will need to determine with your group how long you want to meet each week so you can plan your time accordingly. Generally, most groups like to meet for either sixty minutes or ninety minutes, so you could use one of the following schedules:

Section	60 Minutes	90 Minutes
WELCOME (members arrive and get settled)	5 minutes	10 minutes
REFLECTION (discuss the opening question for the lesson)	10 minutes	15 minutes
DISCUSSION (discuss the Bible study questions in the Exploration and Reaction sections)	35 minutes	50 minutes
PRAYER/CLOSING (pray together as a group and dismiss)	10 minutes	15 minutes

As the group leader, it is up to you to keep track of the time and keep things moving along according to your schedule. You might want to set a timer for each segment so both you and the group members know when your time is up. (Note that there are some good phone apps for timers that play a gentle chime or other pleasant sound instead of a disruptive noise.) Don't feel pressured to cover every question you have selected if the group has a good discussion going. Again, it's not necessary to go around the circle and make everyone share.

Don't be concerned if the group members are silent or slow to share. People are often quiet when they are pulling together their ideas, and this might be a new experience for them. Just ask a question and let it hang in the air until someone shares. You can then say, "Thank you. What about others? What came to you when you reflected on the passage?"

GROUP DYNAMICS

Leading a group through *Life Lessons from Acts* will prove to be highly rewarding both to you and your group members—but that doesn't mean you will not encounter any challenges along the way! Discussions can get off track. Group members may not be sensitive to the needs and ideas of others. Some might worry they will be expected to talk about matters that make them feel awkward. Others may express comments that result in disagreements. To help ease this strain on you and the group, consider the following ground rules:

- When someone raises a question or comment that is off the main topic, suggest you deal with it another time, or, if you feel led to go in that direction, let the group know you will be spending some time discussing it.
- If someone asks a question you don't know how to answer, admit it and move on. At your discretion, feel free to invite group members to comment on questions that call for personal experience.
- If you find one or two people are dominating the discussion time, direct a few questions to others in the group. Outside the main group time, ask the more dominating members to help you draw out the quieter ones. Work to make them a part of the solution instead of the problem.
- When a disagreement occurs, encourage the group members to process the matter in love. Encourage those on opposite sides to restate what they heard the other side say about the matter, and then invite each side to evaluate if that perception is accurate. Lead the group in examining other Scriptures related to the topic and look for common ground.

When any of these issues arise, encourage your group members to follow the words from the Bible: "Love one another" (John 13:34), "If it is possible, as far as it depends on you, live at peace with everyone" (Romans 12:18), and, "Be quick to listen, slow to speak and slow to become angry" (James 1:19).

Thank you again for taking the time to lead your group. May God reward your efforts and dedication and make your time together in this study fruitful for his kingdom.

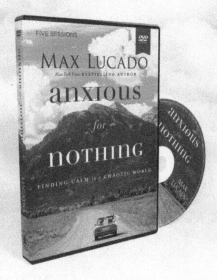

Inspired by what you just read?
Connect with Max.

Listen to Max's teaching ministry, UpWords, on the radio and online. Visit www.MaxLucado.com to get FREE resources for spiritual growth and encouragement, including:

- Archives of UpWords, Max's daily radio program, and a list of radio stations where it airs
- Devotionals and e-mails from Max
- First look at book excerpts
- Downloads of audio, video, and printed material
- Mobile content

You will also find an online store and special offers.

www.MaxLucado.com

1-800-822-9673

UpWords Ministries
P.O. Box 692170
San Antonio, TX 78269-2170

Join the Max Lucado community:

Follow Max on Twitter @MaxLucado
or at Facebook.com/MaxLucado